Making
Wooden Toys

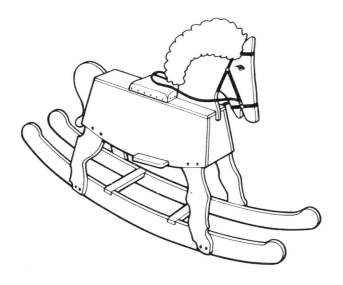

Making Wooden Toys

Richard E. Blizzard

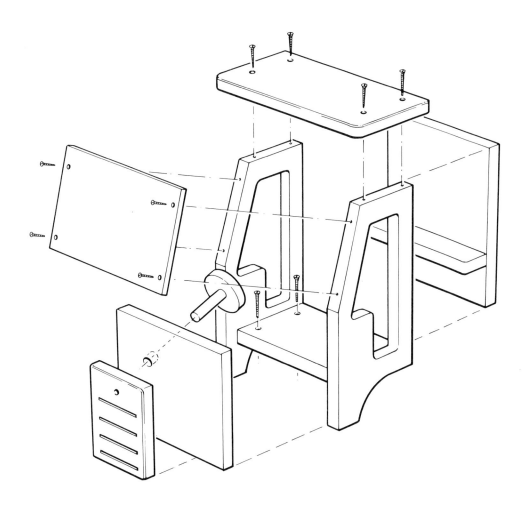

John Murray

© Richard E. Blizzard 1982

First published 1982
by John Murray (Publishers) Ltd
50 Albemarle Street, London W1X 4BD
Reprinted 1983, 1984, 1986
First paperback edition 1993

Printed in Great Britain by
St Edmundsbury Press Ltd, Bury St Edmunds

A catalogue record for this book is available
from the British Library

ISBN 0–7195–5296–6

Contents

Acknowledgements

A special thank you to Jim Dumigham, Marian Foster, Donny MacLeod and my producer Jenny Cowan and all the team who gave me so much encouragement and help with *Wooden Toys From Pebble Mill*; Peter F. Farley and Mervyn Hurford for producing the magnificent drawings without which the book would have been impossible; Edward, Joy and Christopher who tested the toys in prototype; and last, but by no means least, my wife, who listened, helped and encouraged.

Introduction

Of all living plants the tree has probably had more influence on mankind and his development than any other. Early man hollowed out the tree-trunk for his boat and the shaft of his spear came from the tree. He used its dead branches to keep himself warm and fend off the wild beasts.

Not only was timber of use in man's domestic life but later he was to use it for his wheels, siege engines, bows and arrows, bridges, ships and for many years even his aeroplanes. The tree made it possible for man to travel and trade throughout the world.

The tree in its life is a thing of natural beauty giving the beholder a sense of its great strength and graceful shape. Over the centuries craftsmen, designers and architects realised its full potential and their work stands today as a monument to the beauty and versatility of this the largest of all plants.

It therefore followed naturally that children's toys were made from wood. Some were elaborate, made by skilled craftsmen, but perhaps it was the humbler simple-carved toy that held the most appeal, fashioned by the old wood-carver. None knew better than he the true nature of the knarled oak, the gentle ripple to be found in ash, and the dark beauty of walnut.

Working with wood is a continuing source of pleasure as each piece is so different in grain, texture, colour and feel. Each species of wood gives off a scent, some most pleasing, others fresh and clean to smell. Besides, there is a tremendous sense of achievement when using a sharp plane, in watching the tightly packed curls of wood shavings spilling from the tool, to be picked up by small eager fingers, thrilled at this new discovery.

With the introduction of plastics, toys changed from their traditional material and became available in gaudy bright moulded 'bubbles'. However, this useful material has its limitations. After a while scratches make even the treasured plastic tractor scruffy, and many families despair when breakages cannot be repaired. Perhaps worst of all is the resulting sense of disappointment – and toys that let children down are bad toys. The child uses his toys as a means of experiment, with them he learns and discovers many things. To the very young child play and work are inseparable.

I have tried in this book to include both simple and more demanding toys, in the hope that many who have not made wooden toys will attempt to do so and will be encouraged by their efforts to go on and enjoy working in this most precious of materials. I hope that at the end you will have experienced the words of my motto 'I too will something make and joy in the making.'

Richard E. Blizzard

Author's Note

There is no reason why the toys featured in this book should not be adapted and I encourage this to be done. I should like parents and schools to use the ideas just as a starting-point for some design technology.

A basic set of woodworking tools is needed and if you plan to make the more complicated toys some others will be necessary. All the toys featured can be built with normal hand tools. Electric tools will speed up the process and sometimes produce better results but they are not essential.

There are a number of general points which should be noted before attempting to make any of the toys in this book.

Points to Note

1   **Saws** The two essential saws for making the toys in this book are:

1 The tenon saw

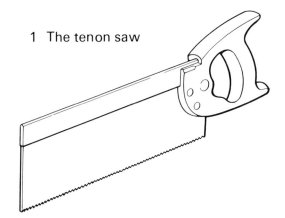

2 The coping saw

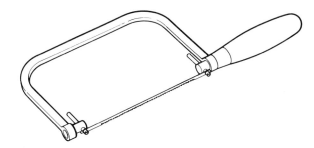

2   **Woods** Throughout this book pine is recommended where plywood is not specified. However for the more ambitious toymaker the use of woods such as beech, oak, ash or mahogany can produce outstanding results and when clear varnished give a beautiful finish.

3 **Glues** Any proprietary brand of wood glue is suitable for use when constructing these toys.

4 **Paint/Varnish** If the toys in this book are painted it is important that *non-toxic* paints and primers are used. These are safe for children and comply with the Toy Safety Regulations. A large range of these paints are available through model shops. Varnish or paint are only listed under specific toys where they are essential for protection for the toy.

5 **Countersinking screws etc.** Throughout it is recommended that all screws and panel pins are countersunk. This is a general rule and is not always specified in the construction sections.

6 **Wheels and axles** Wheels, axles and spring axle clips are sometimes not fully available through model shops. If in difficulty they can be ordered in the U.K. direct from:

> R. Blizzard (Wheels)
> P.O. Box 5
> Gloucester
> GL3 4RJ

Please write with a stamped addressed envelope for a price list. The wheels and axles will be sent immediately on receipt of the necessary remittance.

Depending on availability it may on occasions be necessary to use wheels of slightly different dimensions to those specified in this book. This should pose no problem so long as the axle holes are always measured to fit the axles used. However the central spindle of the Roundabout with Horses, for example, may need to be adjusted in length to suit an alternative wheel dimension.

Axle rods will need to be trimmed to the correct length. Always round axle-rod ends with a file before fitting on the spring clips which hold the wheels in place.

7 **Measurements** Metric measurements always appear first with imperial measurements in brackets after. The measurements in inches are not always exact conversions of the metric measurements but are carefully worked out to suit the specific toys.

Escaping Robber

This villainous character jiggles down the ladder complete with his bag of 'swag'. The design allows all parts to be folded flat after play, or the inevitable arrest.

WALL

FOOT

DO NOT GLUE WALL, STAND OR LADDER TO EACH OTHER. THE TOY MAY THEN BE DISMANTLED FOR STORAGE.

EXTRA THICKNESS OF 9(³⁄₈) PLYWOOD ON EACH SIDE OF SLOT.

Cutting List

HOUSE WALL*	1 off	610 mm (24 in.) × 200 mm ($7\frac{7}{8}$ in.) × 9 mm ($\frac{3}{8}$ in.)
ROOF	1 off	200 mm ($7\frac{7}{8}$ in.) × 70 mm ($2\frac{3}{4}$ in.) × 20 mm ($\frac{3}{4}$ in.)
ROOF	1 off	220 mm ($8\frac{5}{8}$ in.) × 70 mm ($2\frac{3}{4}$ in.) × 20 mm ($\frac{3}{4}$ in.)
CHIMNEY	1 off	70 mm ($2\frac{3}{4}$ in.) × 18 mm ($\frac{3}{4}$ in.) diameter dowel
FOOT*	1 off	650 mm ($25\frac{5}{8}$ in.) × 80 mm ($3\frac{1}{8}$ in.) × 9 mm ($\frac{3}{8}$ in.)
LADDER*	1 off	770 mm ($30\frac{1}{4}$ in.) × 30 mm ($1\frac{1}{8}$ in.) × 9 mm ($\frac{3}{8}$ in.)
ROBBER*	1 off	260 mm ($10\frac{1}{4}$ in.) × 110 mm ($4\frac{3}{8}$ in.) × 9 mm ($\frac{3}{8}$ in.)
DOWEL ROD	4 off	34 mm ($1\frac{3}{8}$ in.) × 5 mm ($\frac{3}{16}$ in.) diameter dowel

*=plywood

Other materials

Screws, plastic tube to pass loosely over 5 mm ($\frac{3}{16}$ in.) dowel rods (optional), small hook and eye for robber's sack, wood glue.

Escaping Robber construction details

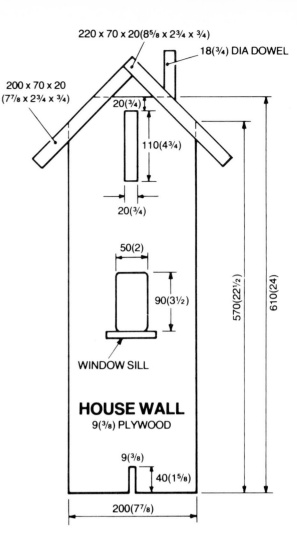

1 Study diagrams and identify pieces.

2 Draw positions of windows on wall of house and secure wall in a vice. Drill a small hole in the corner of top window. Remove one end of coping saw blade from its frame, thread through hole and reattach. Now using saw cut out window.

3 The larger window cannot be cut out in same way (unless a keyhole saw is used) as the 'back' of the coping saw will not clear the top and bottom of the house. Instead secure wall to a firm flat surface and using a chisel cut out window.

4 Add window sill to large window if required using odd off-cut of wood and glue into position.

5 Cut slot in base of wall. This will fit into foot when model is assembled.

6 Cut off top two corners of wall so that edges run at angle of roof as shown.

7 Fit chimney to roof by gluing.

8 Fit roofs to wall, screwing through wall into roof from behind.

9 Now make ladder. Fix wood firmly in a vice and cut zigzags with tenon saw.

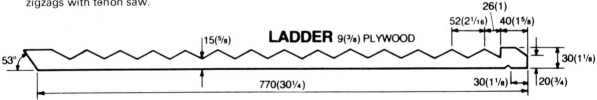

10 Cut a small notch in top underside of ladder to fit over house wall.

11 Sandpaper ladder to remove all roughness.

12 Cut out foot as shown making sure the slot at house end fits securely into slot at base of wall.

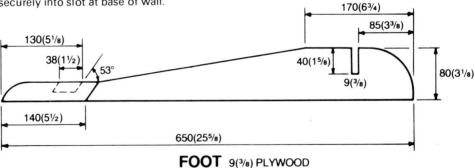

13 Now make socket in foot for base of ladder. First cut out slot and 2 pieces of 9 mm ($\frac{3}{8}$ in.) plywood that sandwich it (see main diagram). Glue these together making sure ladder fits snugly (but is easily removable) before gluing.

16

14 Make cardboard templates of different parts of robber (following gridded diagrams). Transfer shapes on to plywood.

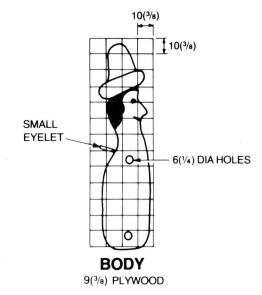

SMALL EYELET

6(¼) DIA HOLES

10(³⁄₈)

10(³⁄₈)

BODY
9(³⁄₈) PLYWOOD

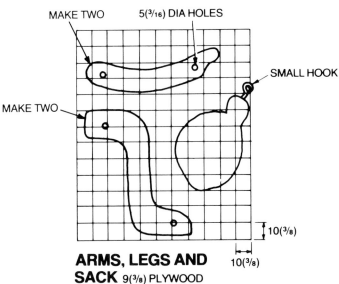

MAKE TWO

5(³⁄₁₆) DIA HOLES

SMALL HOOK

MAKE TWO

10(³⁄₈)

10(³⁄₈)

ARMS, LEGS AND SACK 9(³⁄₈) PLYWOOD

15 First drill all holes. Then cut out body, arms, legs and sack (a coping saw is best for this).

16 Now pass dowel through body and into arms. Glue ends of dowel into arms but allow to pivot freely through body. Follow same procedure for legs.

JOIN ARMS AND LEGS TO BODY WITH DOWELS. GLUE DOWELS TO ARMS AND LEGS, BUT NOT TO BODY.

FIT HARD PLASTIC TUBING OVER DOWELS BETWEEN HANDS AND FEET.

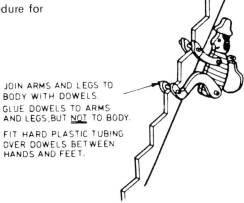

17 Glue pieces of 5 mm ($\frac{3}{16}$ in.) dowel to attach hands and feet. If these pieces of dowel are passed through small lengths of plastic tube which turn freely between the hands and between the feet the robber will move faster down the ladder.

18 The sack is fitted to the robber's back by small hook and eye screws.

19 Assemble complete model. Place robber at top of ladder. He will remain still until touched. He will then race off to the ground.

Paddle Boat

This small paddle boat is perfect for bath and garden pond. The elastic-band motor provides an ideal means of propulsion. This model is easy to make with the minimum of tools. The design of the superstructure and hull can be adapted as required.

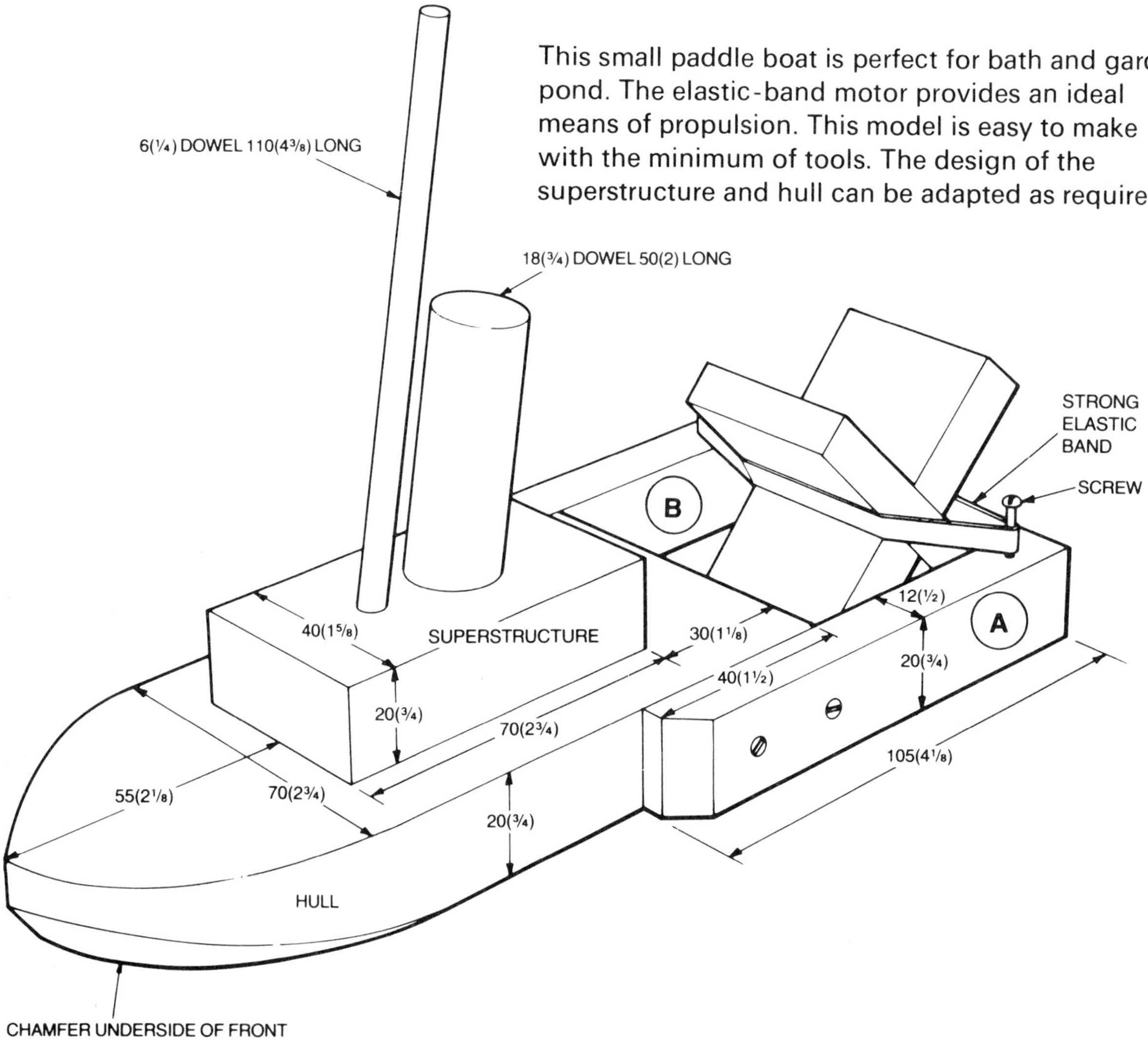

6(1/4) DOWEL 110(4 3/8) LONG
18(3/4) DOWEL 50(2) LONG
STRONG ELASTIC BAND
SCREW
B
A
40(1 5/8)
SUPERSTRUCTURE
30(1 1/8)
12(1/2)
40(1 1/2)
20(3/4)
20(3/4)
70(2 3/4)
105(4 1/8)
55(2 1/8)
70(2 3/4)
20(3/4)
HULL
CHAMFER UNDERSIDE OF FRONT

Cutting List

HULL	1 off	155 mm (6 in.) × 70 mm ($2\frac{3}{4}$ in.) × 20 mm ($\frac{3}{4}$ in.)
SUPER-STRUCTURE	1 off	70 mm ($2\frac{3}{4}$ in.) × 40 mm ($1\frac{5}{8}$ in.) × 20 mm ($\frac{3}{4}$ in.)
FUNNEL	1 off	50 mm (2 in.) × 18 mm ($\frac{3}{4}$ in.) diameter dowel
MAST	1 off	110 mm ($4\frac{3}{8}$ in.) × 6 mm ($\frac{1}{4}$ in.) diameter dowel
PADDLE STAYS	2 off	105 mm ($4\frac{1}{8}$ in.) × 20 mm ($\frac{3}{4}$ in.) × 12 mm ($\frac{1}{2}$ in.)
PADDLE*	2 off	70 mm ($2\frac{3}{4}$ in.) × 36 mm ($1\frac{3}{8}$ in.) × 9 mm ($\frac{3}{8}$ in.)

* = plywood

Other materials

Elastic bands, brass screws, varnish/paint, wood glue.

Paddle Boat
construction details

1   Cut and shape hull as shown.

2   Shape paddle stays A and B and screw on to sides of hull. If possible use brass screws which do not rust.

3   Drill shallow holes at a slight angle in superstructure to hold funnel and mast. Glue funnel and mast in place. Glue superstructure on to hull.

4   Make paddle from 2 pieces of 9 mm ($\frac{3}{8}$ in.) plywood. Cut slot in each with tenon saw removing 'waste' with small chisel. Fit pieces together and glue.

5   Insert two brass screws to hold elastic band. Fit paddle in place. Choose best size of elastic band by experimenting. A strong thick band gives fast acceleration with short range. A thinner band gives slower speed with longer range.

6   Give boat and paddle a good coat of varnish or gloss paint to protect wood from water.

7   Wind up paddle until elastic band is fully stretched. Place boat in water and release.

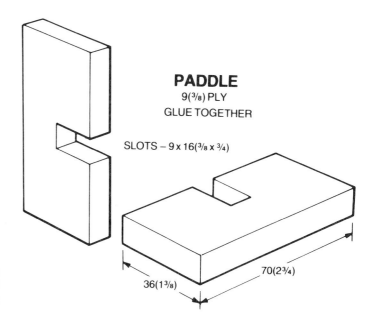

PADDLE
9($\frac{3}{8}$) PLY
GLUE TOGETHER

SLOTS – 9 x 16($\frac{3}{8}$ x $\frac{3}{4}$)

70(2$\frac{3}{4}$)

36(1$\frac{3}{8}$)

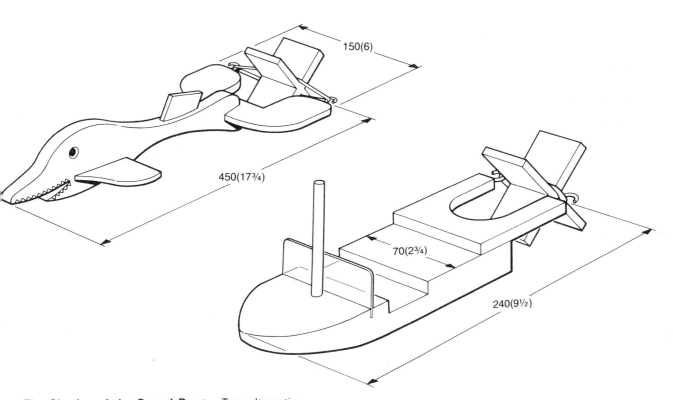

150(6)

450(17$\frac{3}{4}$)

70(2$\frac{3}{4}$)

240(9$\frac{1}{2}$)

The Shark and the Speed Boat – Two alternative designs based on the same method of propulsion.

19

Somersaulting Clown

The rolling action of this clown will hold your attention. Traditionally this toy has a straight inclined ramp. I have added a curved track with stops at the top. With practice you can spin the clown at the bottom and watch him climb to the top where he will rotate and then slowly, very slowly at first, start to run down again. A little chalk rubbed along the tracks will help him to climb smoothly.

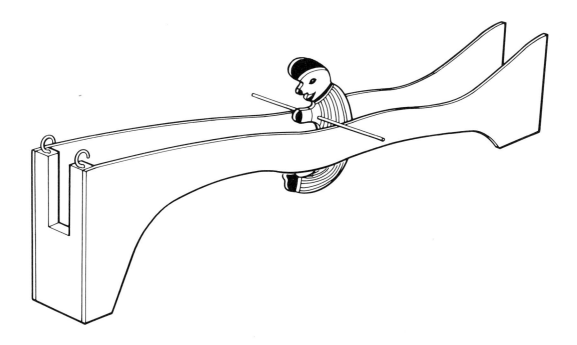

Cutting List

RUNNERS★	2 off	820 mm (2 ft 8½ in.) × 180 mm (7 in.) × 7 mm (¼ in.)
REAR SPACER	1 off	75 mm (3 in.) × 70 mm (2¾ in.) × 20 mm (¾ in.)
FRONT SPACER	1 off	170 mm (6¾ in.) × 70 mm (2¾ in.) × 20 mm (¾ in.)
CLOWN★	1 off	140 mm (5¼ in.) × 140 mm (5¼ in.) × 7 mm (¼ in.)
DOWEL SPINDLE ROD	1 off	180 mm (7 in.) × 5 mm (³⁄₁₆ in.) diameter dowel

★=plywood

Other materials

Two cup hooks, screws, wood glue.

Somersaulting Clown
construction details

1 Transfer shape of runners on to card or paper. Cut out pattern and transfer on to plywood.

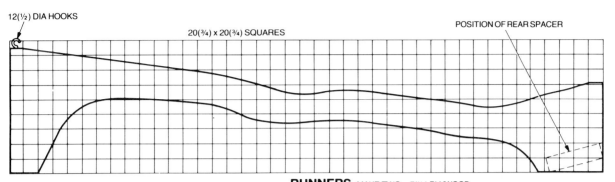

12(½) DIA HOOKS

20(¾) x 20(¾) SQUARES

POSITION OF REAR SPACER

RUNNERS MAKE TWO   7(¼) PLYWOOD

2 Cut out plywood runners with coping saw. Both runners can be cut out in one operation if the two pieces of plywood are firmly clamped together before sawing.

3 Smooth all edges with glasspaper.

4 Cut out spacers which hold runners together. Cut slot in front spacer.

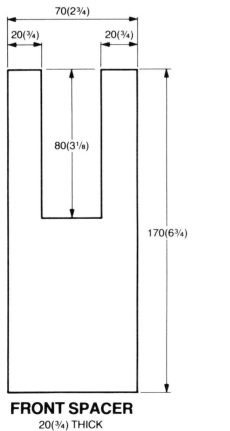

70(2¾)

20(¾)   20(¾)

80(3⅛)

170(6¾)

FRONT SPACER
20(¾) THICK

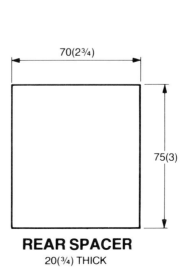

70(2¾)

75(3)

REAR SPACER
20(¾) THICK

21

5   Glue and screw runners to spacers checking alignment carefully.

6   Fix two hooks on front spacer. These catch clown when he reaches the top and return him back to the start.

7   Transfer shape of clown on to card or paper. Cut out pattern and transfer on to plywood. Cut out plywood.

SUGGESTED COLOUR SCHEME

RED   BLACK   WHITE

20(¾) x 20(¾) SQUARES   **CLOWN**   7(¼) PLYWOOD

8   Drill hole in clown and fit dowel spindle rod.

9   Clown must balance correctly. To adjust file head or feet as necessary.

10   Paint clown in bright colours.

11   Rub chalk along runner tracks. The clown can now perform.

DOWEL SPINDLE ROD

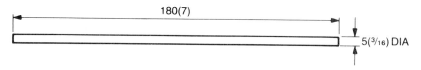

180(7)

5(³/₁₆) DIA

22

Puppet Theatre

All children can enjoy a puppet theatre. It gives great scope for imagination and on its stage their favourite stories and nursery rhymes can come to life.

This theatre is designed to be dismantled and folded flat when not in use.

Cutting List

SIDE PANELS★	2 off	760 mm (29$\frac{7}{8}$ in.) ×294 mm (11$\frac{5}{8}$ in.) ×9 mm ($\frac{3}{8}$ in.)
TOP AND BOTTOM PANELS★	2 off	1220 mm (48 in.) ×170 mm (6$\frac{3}{4}$ in.) ×9 mm ($\frac{3}{8}$ in.)
BACK PANEL★	1 off	1020 mm (40$\frac{1}{8}$ in.) ×600 mm (23$\frac{5}{8}$ in.) ×9 mm ($\frac{3}{8}$ in.)
STAGE★	1 off	1220 mm (48 in.) ×250 mm (9$\frac{7}{8}$ in.) ×9 mm ($\frac{3}{8}$ in.)

★=plywood

Other materials

Two small plastic jointing blocks and screws, curtain track, material for curtains, curtain hooks.

Puppet Theatre
construction details

General Instruction: All slots in the panels are 9 mm (⅜ in.) wide. It is essential that the width is always correct so that the parts fit firmly together.

If you wish to make a finger puppet theatre halve all dimensions (except width of slots).

Cut out the 2 side panels and cut slots as shown.

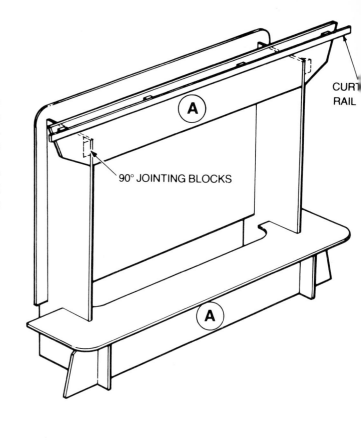

CURT
RAIL

90° JOINTING BLOCKS

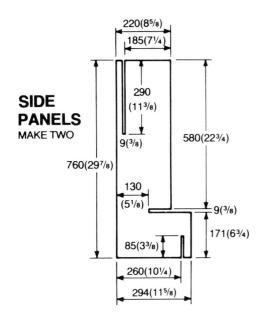

SIDE PANELS
MAKE TWO

220(8⅝)
185(7¼)
290 (11⅜)
9(⅜)
580(22¾)
760(29⅞)
130 (5⅛)
9(⅜)
171(6¾)
85(3⅜)
260(10¼)
294(11⅝)

2   Now cut out the two A panels and back panel.

PANELS Ⓐ   MAKE TWO

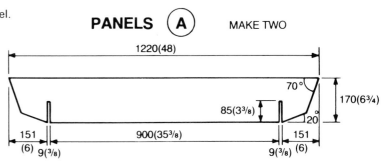

1220(48)
70°
170(6¾)
85(3⅜)
20°
151
(6)
9(⅜)
900(35⅜)
9(⅜)
151
(6)

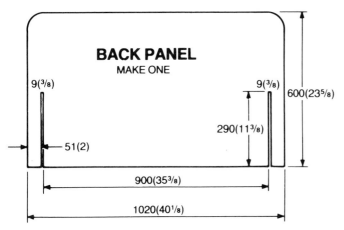

BACK PANEL
MAKE ONE

9(⅜)
9(⅜)
600(23⅝)
290(11⅜)
51(2)
900(35⅜)
1020(40⅛)

24

3   Cut out stage. If large puppets are to be used the width of the stage can be reduced to allow more room between back panel and back edge of stage.

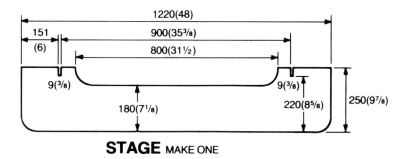

STAGE MAKE ONE

4   Before assembling theatre all slots will need to be 'eased' so that they fit smoothly and firmly. To do this use a piece of glass paper wrapped round a steel ruler. Try out each pair of slots separately. They must make a good tight fit. Rubbing a little candle wax on the edges of each slot helps greatly.

5   Fit the length of curtain track on to the front fascia board (top panel A) as shown.

6   Assemble theatre. To give the panel holding the curtain track greater strength, attach this to the side panels by screwing on small plastic jointing blocks. These will be the only screws that need to be removed when dismantling theatre.

7   Add curtains and the theatre is ready. Scenery can be painted on to sheets of paper which can be clipped in turn on to back panel for effect.

8   There are many books on how to make puppets. However a useful one on simple puppets is published by Ladybird Books Ltd in the 'How to Make' series 633 *Puppets*. This shows methods of making puppets from readily available household materials.

Sand Engine

This little machine will provide hours of enjoyment. The hopper at the top is filled with sand which pours through a small hole and turns the paddle wheel. A spoon provides an ideal shovel to refill the hopper.

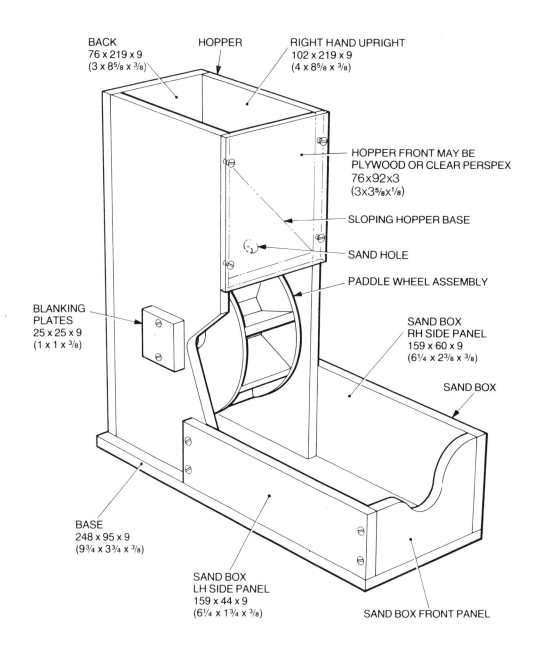

BACK
76 x 219 x 9
(3 x 8⅝ x ⅜)

HOPPER

RIGHT HAND UPRIGHT
102 x 219 x 9
(4 x 8⅝ x ⅜)

HOPPER FRONT MAY BE PLYWOOD OR CLEAR PERSPEX
76x92x3
(3x3⅝x⅛)

SLOPING HOPPER BASE

SAND HOLE

PADDLE WHEEL ASSEMBLY

BLANKING PLATES
25 x 25 x 9
(1 x 1 x ⅜)

SAND BOX
RH SIDE PANEL
159 x 60 x 9
(6¼ x 2⅜ x ⅜)

SAND BOX

BASE
248 x 95 x 9
(9¾ x 3¾ x ⅜)

SAND BOX
LH SIDE PANEL
159 x 44 x 9
(6¼ x 1¾ x ⅜)

SAND BOX FRONT PANEL

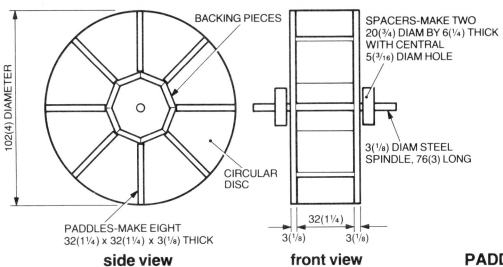

**side view
(one disc removed to show paddles)**

front view

**PADDLE WHEEL
ASSEMBLY**

Cutting List

UPRIGHTS (to hold wheel)★	2 off	219 mm (8⅝ in.) × 102 mm (4 in.) × 9 mm (⅜ in.)
BACK★	1 off	219 mm (8⅝ in.) × 76 mm (3 in.) × 9 mm (⅜ in.)
HOPPER FRONT (plywood or perspex)	1 off	92 mm (3⅝ in.) × 76 mm (3 in.) × 3 mm (⅛ in.)
SANDBOX (right hand side panel★)	1 off	159 mm (6¼ in.) × 60 mm (2⅜ in.) × 9 mm (⅜ in.)
SANDBOX (left hand side panel★)	1 off	159 mm (6¼ in.) × 44 mm (1¾ in.) × 9 mm (⅜ in.)
BASE★	1 off	248 mm (9¾ in.) × 95 mm (3¾ in.) × 9 mm (⅜ in.)
BLANKING PLATES★	2 off	25 mm (1 in.) × 25 mm (1 in.) × 9 mm (⅜ in.)
SANDBOX (front panel★)	1 off	76 mm (3 in.) × 60 mm (2⅜ in.) × 9 mm (⅜ in.)
HOPPER BASE★	1 off	111 mm (4⅜ in.) × 76 mm (3 in.) × 9 mm (⅜ in.)
PADDLE-WHEEL SIDES★	2 off	102 mm (4 in.) × 102 mm (4 in.) × 9 mm (⅜ in.)
PADDLES★	8 off	32 mm (1¼ in.) × 32 mm (1¼ in.) × 3 mm (⅛ in.)
BACKING PIECES★ (cut from one strip)	1 off	205 mm (8 in.) × 32 mm (1¼ in.) × 3 mm (⅛ in.)

★=plywood

Other materials

Axle (which can be made from a steel knitting-needle),
screws and wood glue.

Sand Engine
construction details

1   Mark out 2 discs to form paddle-wheel sides. Cut out with coping saw. (For details of how to cut out a disc see Roundabout with Horses construction detail 14 page 41.)

2   Clamp the two discs together and drill axle hole. 'The axle can be made from a steel knitting-needle. Select axle before drilling hole in order to match sizes.

3   The 8 paddles inside the wheel are all identical. Cut these from a strip of plywood. There must be *no* variation in width otherwise the wheel will not assemble accurately.

4   Cut 8 small backing pieces to fit behind each paddle. These prevent sand from entering centre of wheel.

5   Assemble wheel by gluing paddles and backing pieces on to one disc. Then glue second disc into place. Push axle through axle hole to align both discs correctly before glue sets. Alighment must be carefully checked or wheel will turn unevenly.

6   Cut out the back and 2 sides (uprights) of wheel box. Clamp sides together and drill axle hole.

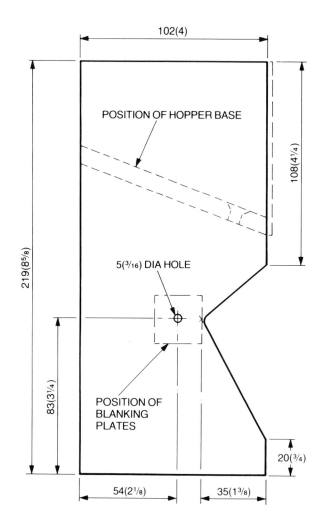

102(4)

POSITION OF HOPPER BASE

108(4¼)

219(8⅝)

5(³/₁₆) DIA HOLE

83(3¼)

POSITION OF
BLANKING
PLATES

20(¾)

54(2⅛)   35(1⅜)

LEFT HAND UPRIGHT
9(³/₈) PLYWOOD

7   Glue and screw sides to back.

8   Cut hopper base and drill small sand hole as shown. The size of sand hole depends on fineness of sand used. The hole must be large enough for sand to run smoothly through it.

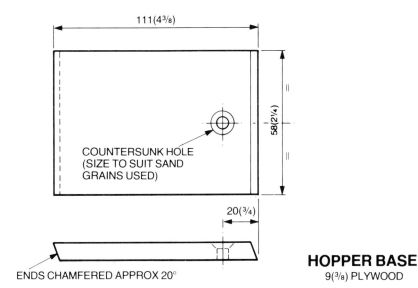

111(4³/₈)

58(2¹/₄)

COUNTERSUNK HOLE
(SIZE TO SUIT SAND
GRAINS USED)

20(³/₄)

ENDS CHAMFERED APPROX 20°

HOPPER BASE
9(³/₈) PLYWOOD

9   Glue hopper base into position making sure it fits tightly. Hopper base slopes to allow sand to slide down and pass through sand hole.

10 Cut out front panel of sand box and glue and screw side panels to it.

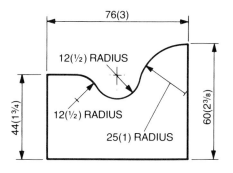

76(3)

12(¹/₂) RADIUS

44(1³/₄)

12(¹/₂) RADIUS

60(2³/₈)

25(1) RADIUS

SAND BOX FRONT PANEL
9(³/₈) PLYWOOD

11 Glue and screw sand box to wheel box as shown.

12 Glue and screw single piece base to wheel box and sand box.

13 Cut wheel axle to length so it does not protrude on either side of sand engine box. Then fit wheel in place inserting spacers as shown on paddle-wheel assembly diagram. To prevent axle coming out screw a small square of plywood (blanking plate) over each axle hole.

14 The Sand Engine should be painted or varnished to ensure long life.

15 Fill hopper box with fine sand and the wheel will start turning.

Sand Digger

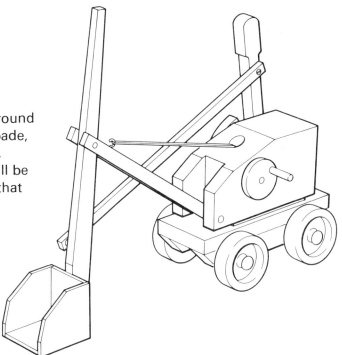

Watch any group of young children clustered around the sand pit or on the beach with bucket and spade, totally absorbed in the creative work of digging, building, smoothing and tunnelling, and you will be in no doubt that this small machine will add to that enjoyment.

Cutting List

CHASSIS SIDE PIECES	2 off	220 mm ($8\frac{5}{8}$ in.) × 25 mm (1 in.) × 20 mm ($\frac{3}{4}$ in.)
CHASSIS PLATFORM	1 off	220 mm ($8\frac{5}{8}$ in.) × 80 mm ($3\frac{1}{8}$ in.) × 20 mm ($\frac{3}{4}$ in.)
HARDBOARD	1 off	120 mm ($4\frac{3}{4}$ in.) × 60 mm ($2\frac{3}{8}$ in.) × 3 mm ($\frac{1}{8}$ in.)
CAB	1 off	180 mm (7 in.) × 94 mm ($3\frac{3}{4}$ in.) × 70 mm ($2\frac{3}{4}$ in.)
BUCKET★	1 off	330 mm (13 in.) × 82 mm ($3\frac{1}{4}$ in.) × 6 mm ($\frac{1}{4}$ in.)
WINDING HANDLE DISC	1 off	50 mm (2 in.) × 50 mm (2 in.) × 9 mm ($\frac{3}{8}$ in.)
RATCHET AND PAWL★	1 off	45 mm ($1\frac{3}{4}$ in.) × 51 mm (2 in.) × 6 mm ($\frac{1}{4}$ in.)
PUSH ROD	1 off	332 mm (13 in.) × 12 mm ($\frac{1}{2}$ in.) × 8 mm ($\frac{3}{8}$ in.)
DIGGER ARM	1 off	365 mm ($14\frac{3}{8}$ in.) × 30 mm ($1\frac{1}{8}$ in.) × 15 mm ($\frac{5}{8}$ in.)
JIB	1 off	240 mm ($9\frac{1}{2}$ in.) × 34 mm ($1\frac{3}{8}$ in.) × 18 mm ($\frac{3}{4}$ in.)
HANDLE	1 off	188 mm ($7\frac{3}{8}$ in.) × 20 mm ($\frac{3}{4}$ in.) × 20 mm ($\frac{3}{4}$ in.)
DOWEL ROD (for winding handle shaft, jib pivot, etc.)	1 off	275 mm (11 in.) × 6 mm ($\frac{1}{4}$ in.) diameter dowel

★ = plywood

Other materials

Four 76 mm (3 in.) diameter wheels, 2 axles, 4 spring axle clips, panel pins, nylon cord, screws, washers, wood glue, varnish or paint.

Sand Digger
construction details

1 First prepare the 2 side pieces that hold wheels on to chassis platform.

2 Clamp them together and drill holes for axles.

3 Push axles through holes to check that they fit and then screw side pieces on to chassis platform.

4 Glue the piece of hardboard rough side down on to top of chassis platform. This will allow cab to swivel smoothly.

5 Drill hole through chassis platform to take the 64 mm ($2\frac{1}{2}$ in.) screw that holds cab to chassis platform.

6 A spring washer under the screw head will prevent the cab becoming loose after initial tightening.

7 The cab is made from a large block of wood. Mark on block (in pencil) position of the various holes and front slot.

8 The sides of front slot are cut with tenon saw. The back of slot is then cut using a coping saw. A chisel is used to tidy up.

9 The hole must now be drilled for the 6 mm ($\frac{1}{4}$ in.) dowel rod which acts as anchor and pivot point for the jib. Each side should be marked and drilled separately.

10 Now using a large drill (a flat bit as used in electric drills is ideal) bore a 20 mm ($\frac{3}{4}$ in.) diameter hole 53 mm (2 in.) deep in top of cab to take nylon cord for raising and lowering jib.

11 Drill hole through side to take winding handle shaft. This hole will pierce the large hole already bored in top of cab.

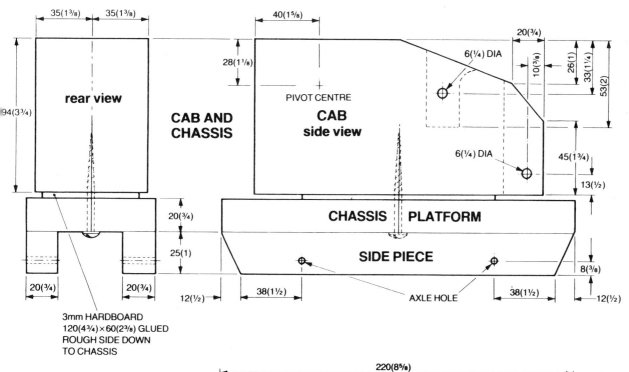

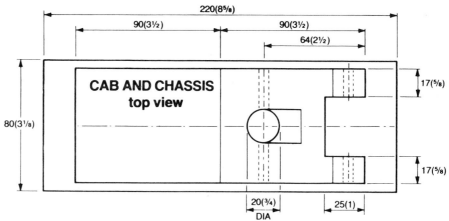

12 Make the little ratchet and pawl from 6 mm ($\frac{1}{4}$ in.)
plywood. These are best cut using a coping saw.

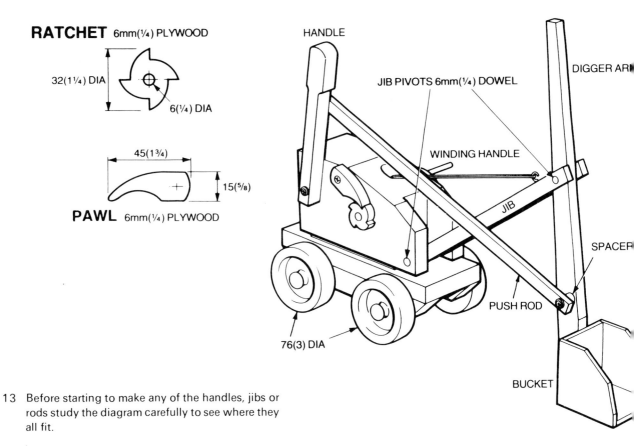

RATCHET 6mm(¼) PLYWOOD

32(1¼) DIA

6(¼) DIA

45(1¾)

15(⅝)

PAWL 6mm(¼) PLYWOOD

HANDLE

JIB PIVOTS 6mm(¼) DOWEL

WINDING HANDLE

DIGGER ARM

JIB

SPACER

PUSH ROD

BUCKET

76(3) DIA

13 Before starting to make any of the handles, jibs or
rods study the diagram carefully to see where they
all fit.

14 Now make winding handle. The circular disc from
9 mm ($\frac{3}{8}$ in.) plywood. The handle and shaft from
6 mm ($\frac{1}{4}$ in.) dowel rod. Drill a fine hole through
shaft to take cord for raising and lowering jib arm.

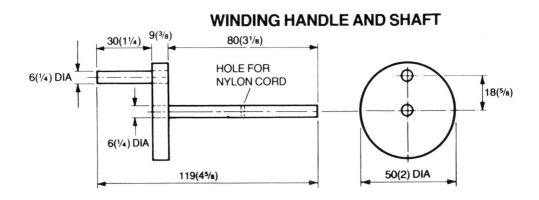

WINDING HANDLE AND SHAFT

30(1¼)   9(³/₈)   80(3⅛)

6(¼) DIA

HOLE FOR
NYLON CORD

6(¼) DIA

119(4⅝)

18(⅝)

50(2) DIA

15 Insert winding handle shaft through bore hole in
cab and make sure it turns freely. If not polish it
with glass paper until it does.

16 Fit and glue ratchet on protruding end of winding
handle shaft. The pawl is then screwed on to cab
loose enough to drop freely into ratchet.

17 Now make jib cutting slot and drilling holes as
    shown.

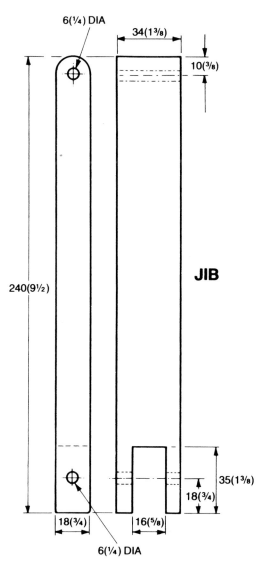

6(¼) DIA
34(1⅜)
10(⅜)

JIB

240(9½)

35(1⅜)
18(¾)

18(¾)
16(⅝)

6(¼) DIA

18 Make handle and screw on to cab. Use a fairly long
    screw, placing a flat washer under head and
    between handle shaft and cab. Washers are used
    in the same way for attaching push rod to handle.

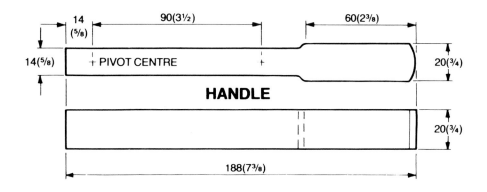

14
(⅝)
90(3½)
60(2⅜)

14(⅝)
+ PIVOT CENTRE   +
20(¾)

HANDLE

20(¾)

188(7⅜)

19 The push rod connects digger arm to handle. Do
    not forget the spacer between push rod and digger
    arm. This can be made from a square or round
    piece of spare plywood.

20 Make bucket from 6 mm ($\frac{1}{4}$ in.) plywood. The sides
    and back are glued and panel pinned in place.

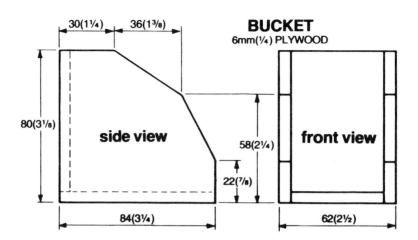

21 Make digger arm. Screw and glue bucket to it.

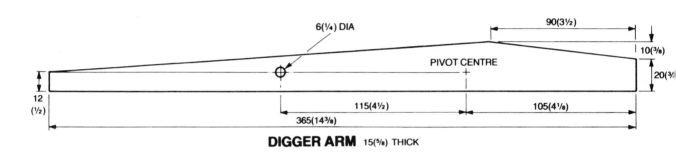

22 Fix digger arm to jib and push rod.

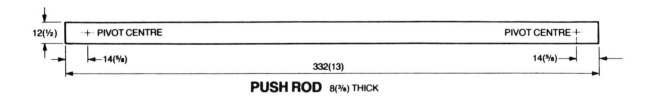

23 Fit nylon cord (or string) to jib arm with small eye
    screw. Attach other end through hole in top of cab
    to shaft of winding handle.

24 Fix axles and wheels.

25 Sand digger is ready for use. The digging action is
    carried out by pushing handle forwards and
    backwards. The height is controlled by winding
    handle which is locked in place by ratchet.

Snooker (Pool) Game

This game can be made as large and as difficult as you wish. For children the sizes given here are ideal but a longer board with more holes and deflectors makes the game a greater challenge.

The walls and deflector boards can be removed and laid flat when the game is not in use.

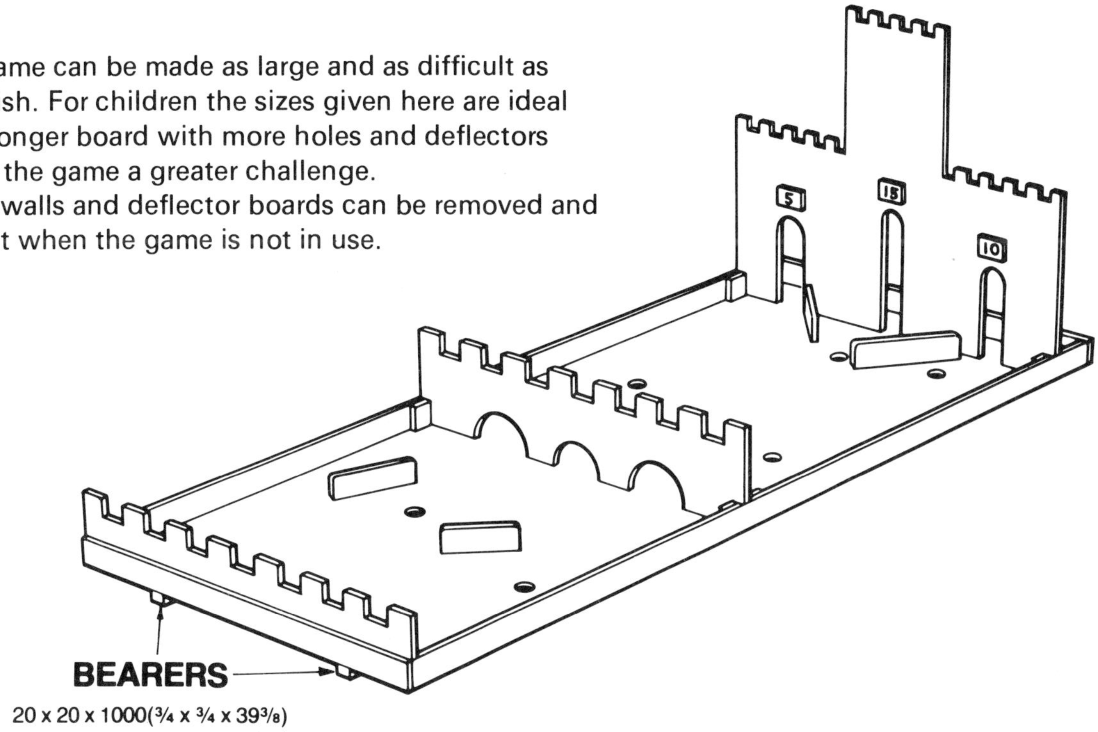
5
15
10
BEARERS
20 x 20 x 1000(3/4 x 3/4 x 39 3/8)

Cutting List

THE BASE*	1 off	1000 mm ($39\frac{3}{8}$ in.) × 402 mm ($15\frac{3}{4}$ in.) × 9 mm ($\frac{3}{8}$ in.)
THE SIDE WALLS*	2 off	1000 mm ($39\frac{3}{8}$ in.) × 26 mm (1 in.) × 9 mm ($\frac{3}{8}$ in.)
THE END WALLS*	2 off	420 mm ($16\frac{1}{2}$ in.) × 26 mm (1 in.) × 9 mm ($\frac{3}{8}$ in.)
WOOD FOR DEFLECTOR BOARDS*	1 off	630 mm ($24\frac{1}{4}$ in.) × 35 mm ($1\frac{3}{8}$ in.) × 9 mm ($\frac{3}{8}$ in.)
CUES	2 off	800 mm ($31\frac{1}{2}$ in.) × 13 mm ($\frac{1}{2}$ in.) diameter dowel
REAR WALL*	1 off	420 mm ($16\frac{1}{2}$ in.) × 335 mm ($13\frac{1}{8}$ in.) × 9 mm ($\frac{3}{8}$ in.)
CENTRE WALL*	1 off	420 mm ($16\frac{1}{2}$ in.) × 105 mm ($4\frac{1}{8}$ in.) × 9 mm ($\frac{3}{8}$ in.)
FRONT WALL*	1 off	420 mm ($16\frac{1}{2}$ in.) × 70 mm ($2\frac{3}{4}$ in.) × 9 mm ($\frac{3}{8}$ in.)
BEARERS	2 off	1000 mm ($39\frac{3}{8}$ in.) × 20 mm ($\frac{3}{4}$ in.) × 20 mm ($\frac{3}{4}$ in.)
DOWEL ROD (for deflector board pegs)	1 off	135 mm (12 in.) × 6 mm ($\frac{1}{4}$ in.) diameter dowel

* = plywood

Other materials

Fablon baize, screws, glue, marbles.

PLAN VIEW ON BOARD

REAR WALL   CENTRE WALL   FRONT WALL

LOCATING BLOCKS FOR
CASTLE WALLS
26 x 26 x 9(1 x 1 x ³/₈)

SIDE EDGE MEMBERS
1000 x 35 x 9(39³/₈ x 1³/₈ x ³/₈)

ALL HOLES 20(³/₄) DIAMETER
OR TO SUIT MARBLES USED

60(2³/₈)   90(3¹/₂)   170(6⁵/₈)   80(3¹/₈)   140(5¹/₂)   65(2¹/₂)   170(6⁵/₈)   220(8⁵/₈)

200(7⁷/₈)   190(7¹/₂)   30(1¹/₈)   45°   45°

110(4³/₈)   45°   130(5¹/₈) LONG   130(5¹/₈) LONG   70(2³/₄) LONG   230(9)

105(4¹/₈)   80(3¹/₈) LONG   90(3¹/₂)   270(10⁵/₈)

220(8⁵/₈)   45°   130(5¹/₈) LONG   20(³/₄)   90(3¹/₂) LONG   250(9⁷/₈)

105(4¹/₈)   45°   145(5³/₄)   20°   402(15³/₄)

85(3³/₈)   70(2³/₄)

70(2³/₄)   170(6⁵/₈)   440(17³/₈)

940(37)

1000(39³/₈)

END EDGE MEMBERS
420 x 35 x 9(16¹/₂ x 1³/₈ x ³/₈)

Snooker Game construction details

1   Start by cutting base board to size.

2   Now cut out side and end walls. Fix these to base with glue and screws.

3   Turn base over and screw the two bearers in place 25 mm (1 in.) in from each side. These allow marbles to drop through holes and roll out when board is fully assembled.

4   Turn base back over and mark in pencil positions of marble holes. Drill holes 20 mm ($\frac{3}{4}$ in.) diameter or to suit marbles used. These holes must be drilled carefully so wood does not tear. A flat bit in an electric drill is best.

5   After drilling holes use glass paper to remove all rough edges.

6   Now make deflector boards inserting dowel pegs as shown. The number and lengths of deflectors are shown on plan view diagram.

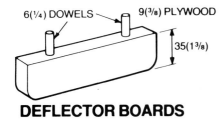

6(¹/₄) DOWELS   9(³/₈) PLYWOOD

35(1³/₈)

DEFLECTOR BOARDS

7   The cues are made from dowel rod. Round ends to prevent cues tearing baize.

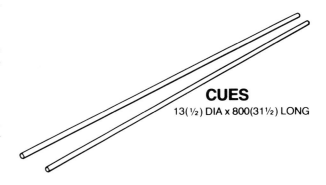

CUES
13(¹/₂) DIA x 800(31¹/₂) LONG

8   Baize for surface is a Fablon product used commercially for lining inside of cutlery boxes. It can be found in large Do-It-Yourself stores.

9   Check base surface is clean and smooth. Cut baize to size with backing on. Peel off backing and stick baize on to board. With sharp craft knife cut round marble holes. It is essential knife is sharp otherwise the edges will be ragged and will spoil smooth run of marbles.

10   Carefully drill deflector board peg holes in base board so deflectors fit in positions shown on plan view diagram.

11 Next cut out castle walls. The castellations are cut with tenon and coping saws. The tenon saw for the vertical cuts, the coping saw for the horizontal cuts. Use coping saw for doorways.

12 Cut and shape 3 small blocks for score cards above doors. Paint on numbers. The narrower (and more difficult) the door, the higher the score. Fix above doors with glue.

13 So that the game can be stored flat, glue small wooden blocks to side walls leaving 9 mm ($\frac{3}{8}$ in.) gaps to allow walls to be slotted in as shown.

14 When assembled the game is ready to play.

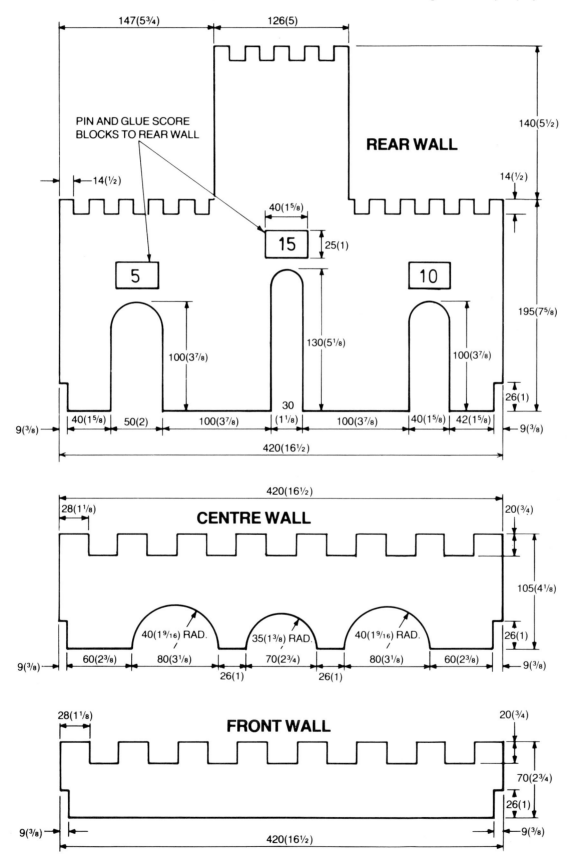

Roundabout (Merry-Go-Round) with Horses

Children are fascinated by things with moving parts. While pushing or pulling this roundabout they will enjoy watching the horses turn round and gently swing outwards. A brightly painted spiral on the top will add to the enjoyment of this toy.

The roundabout is turned by only one of the wheels and there are no cogs to break.

Cutting List

CHASSIS STRIPS	2 off	178 mm (7 in.) × 28 mm ($1\frac{1}{8}$ in.) × 20 mm ($\frac{3}{4}$ in.)
CHASSIS PLATFORM★	1 off	178 mm (7 in.) × 146 mm ($5\frac{3}{4}$ in.) × 6 mm ($\frac{1}{4}$ in.)
MOUNTING BLOCK FOR CENTRAL SPINDLE	1 off	146 mm ($5\frac{3}{4}$ in.) × 44 mm ($1\frac{3}{4}$ in.) × 16 mm ($\frac{5}{8}$ in.)
FRONT AXLE BLOCK	1 off	89 mm ($3\frac{1}{2}$ in.) × 44 mm ($1\frac{3}{4}$ in.) × 20 mm ($\frac{3}{4}$ in.)
FRONT AXLE SIDE PLATES★	2 off	44 mm ($1\frac{3}{4}$ in.) × 41 mm ($1\frac{5}{8}$ in.) × 6 mm ($\frac{1}{4}$ in.)
HANDLE	1 off	406 mm (16 in.) × 25 mm (1 in.) × 20 mm ($\frac{3}{4}$ in.)
DOWEL SPINDLE (for handle)	1 off	44 mm ($1\frac{3}{4}$ in.) × 6 mm ($\frac{1}{4}$ in.) dowel rod
UPPER ROUNDABOUT DISC★	1 off	184 mm ($7\frac{1}{4}$ in.) × 184 mm ($7\frac{1}{4}$ in.) × 6 mm ($\frac{1}{4}$ in.)
LOWER ROUNDABOUT DISC★	1 off	197 mm ($7\frac{3}{4}$ in.) × 197 mm ($7\frac{3}{4}$ in.) × 6 mm ($\frac{1}{4}$ in.)
HORSES★	3 off	200 mm ($7\frac{7}{8}$ in.) × 180 mm (7 in.) × 6 mm ($\frac{1}{4}$ in.)
TOP ROUNDABOUT SPINDLE DISC★	1 off	57 mm ($2\frac{1}{4}$ in.) × 57 mm ($2\frac{1}{4}$ in.) × 6 mm ($\frac{1}{4}$ in.)
CENTRE ROUNDABOUT SPINDLE	1 off	238 mm ($9\frac{3}{8}$ in.) × 12 mm ($\frac{1}{2}$ in.) diameter dowel
ROUNDABOUT PILLARS	3 off	213 mm ($8\frac{3}{8}$ in.) × 9 mm ($\frac{3}{8}$ in.) diameter dowel

★ = plywood

Other materials

Two 83 mm ($3\frac{1}{4}$ in.) wheels, axle and 2 spring axle clips.
One 28 mm ($1\frac{1}{8}$ in.) wheel and axle, screws, wood glue and
nylon cord.

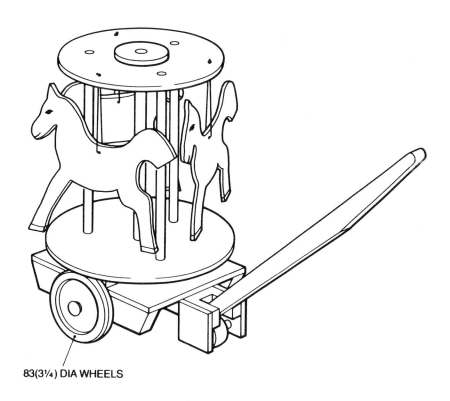

83($3\frac{1}{4}$) DIA WHEELS

Roundabout with Horses
construction details

1   Before starting work study the diagrams and
    identify all the pieces. This will help avoid mistakes
    during construction.

2   First build the chassis. Shape the 2 chassis strips,
    drill a hole for the axle through each as shown and
    screw them to plywood chassis platform.

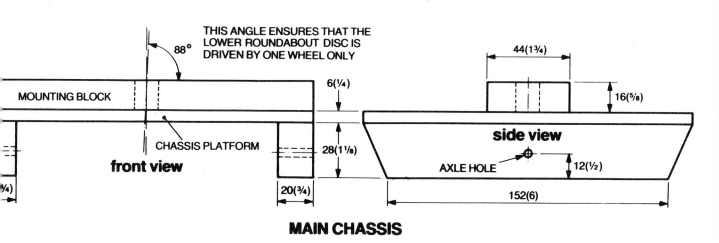

88°

THIS ANGLE ENSURES THAT THE
LOWER ROUNDABOUT DISC IS
DRIVEN BY ONE WHEEL ONLY

6(¼)

MOUNTING BLOCK

44(1¾)

16(⅝)

CHASSIS PLATFORM

side view

28(1⅛)

front view

AXLE HOLE

12(½)

¾)

20(¾)

152(6)

MAIN CHASSIS

3   If the roundabout is to work smoothly the next stage is vital. By studying both the chassis top view diagram and main chassis diagram you will see that the mounting block has a 12 mm ($\frac{1}{2}$ in.) hole drilled through it at an angle of 88°. The hole takes the centre roundabout spindle, and offsets the whole roundabout so that the bottom roundabout disc touches only one wheel. The angle can be increased a little to ensure successful working of toy but not too much or roundabout will look lop-sided.

Now drill hole in mounting block.

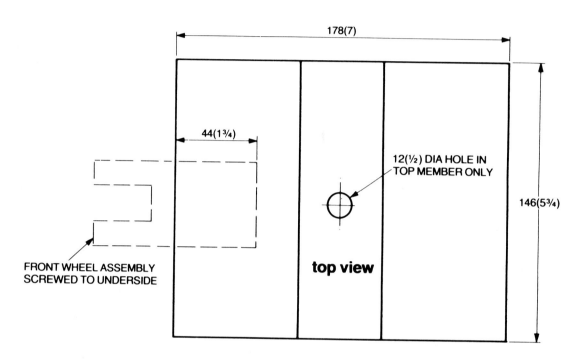

178(7)

44(1¾)

12(½) DIA HOLE IN
TOP MEMBER ONLY

146(5¾)

FRONT WHEEL ASSEMBLY
SCREWED TO UNDERSIDE

top view

4   Glue and screw mounting block on to chassis platform.

5   To balance roundabout a small wheel is mounted at front in a small front axle block.

6   Front axle block also provides anchorage point for handle. Cut out front axle block and drill hole as shown.

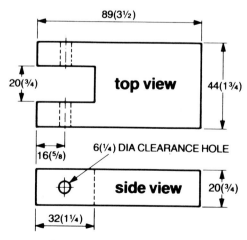

89(3½)

20(¾)   **top view**   44(1¾)

16(⅝)

6(¼) DIA CLEARANCE HOLE

side view   20(¾)

32(1¼)

FRONT AXLE BLOCK

7   Cut out handle and shape as shown and smooth with glass paper. Drill hole.

8   Handle is attached to front axle block by a 44 mm (1¾ in.) long 6 mm (¼ in.) dowel rod. Make sure handle pivots freely in block before gluing dowel rod in place. Dowel must not protrude on either side of block.

9   Drill holes into front axle side plates. These do not go right through side plates as they must hold axle firmly in place.

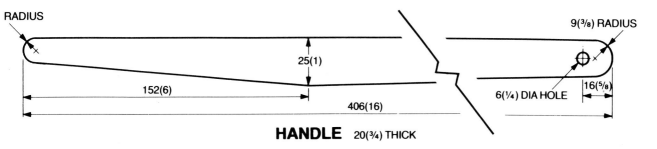

RADIUS

25(1)

152(6)

406(16)

9(³⁄₈) RADIUS

6(¼) DIA HOLE

16(⁵⁄₈)

HANDLE 20(¾) THICK

10 Fit axle and wheel. Plastic tubes make good spacers to keep little wheel in centre of axle.

11 Screw side plates on to front axle block.

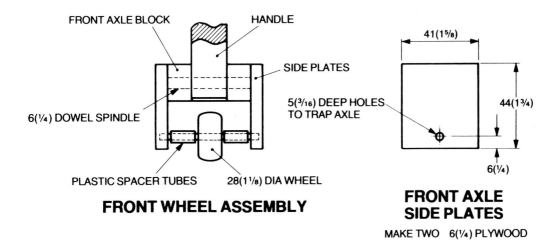

FRONT AXLE BLOCK   HANDLE

SIDE PLATES

6(¼) DOWEL SPINDLE

PLASTIC SPACER TUBES   28(1⅛) DIA WHEEL

FRONT WHEEL ASSEMBLY

41(1⁵⁄₈)

5(³⁄₁₆) DEEP HOLES TO TRAP AXLE

44(1¾)

6(¼)

FRONT AXLE SIDE PLATES

MAKE TWO 6(¼) PLYWOOD

12 Screw front wheel assembly to main chassis.

13 Now prepare the 2 roundabout discs. Mark clearly with a compass the 2 different-sized circles on 2 separate pieces of plywood. Mark in pencil positions of all holes.

14 Cutting out circles in plywood is not difficult:
    (i) Fix plywood firmly in vice and using coping saw start cutting round, following pencil mark. The handle on coping saw will turn, which helps you follow curve.
    (ii) Do not attempt to cut more than a quarter of the circle each time. Keep moving wood in vice and saw as close to vice as possible where plywood is held firmest.
    (iii) When finished smooth circumference of disc carefully with glass paper.
    Repeat method for second disc.

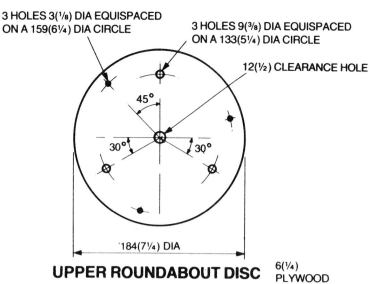

3 HOLES 3(⅛) DIA EQUISPACED
ON A 159(6¼) DIA CIRCLE

3 HOLES 9(⅜) DIA EQUISPACED
ON A 133(5¼) DIA CIRCLE

12(½) CLEARANCE HOLE

45°

30° 30°

184(7¼) DIA

UPPER ROUNDABOUT DISC 6(¼) PLYWOOD

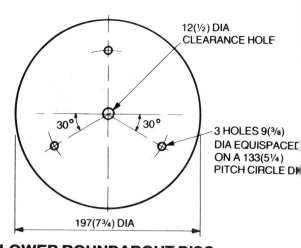

12(½) DIA
CLEARANCE HOLE

30° 30°

3 HOLES 9(⅜)
DIA EQUISPACED
ON A 133(5¼)
PITCH CIRCLE D

197(7¾) DIA

LOWER ROUNDABOUT DISC
6(¼) PLYWOOD

**NOTE: THESE DISCS MUST ROTATE FREELY
ON THE CENTRAL ROUNDABOUT SPINDLE**

15 Drill centre hole in each disc.

16 Place the 2 discs together with centre holes lined
up. Tape discs together in this position at edges.

17 With the 2 discs together drill the larger holes for
roundabout pillars. By drilling discs together the
holes will line up accurately.

18 Next drill 3 smaller holes in upper disc only.
Diameter of holes depends on size of cord used to
hold horses.

19 Cut 3 equal lengths of dowel rod for roundabout
pillars. Push pillars into holes in upper and lower
discs. Always fit pieces together first without glue
to check correct fit.

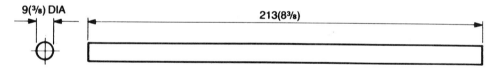

9(⅜) DIA

213(8⅜)

ROUNDABOUT PILLARS   MAKE THREE
**NOTE: GLUE ENDS FLUSH WITH TOP FACE OF UPPER ROUNDABOUT
DISC AND LOWER FACE OF LOWER ROUNDABOUT DISC**

20 Glue pillars in position. Ends must be flush with
top face of upper disc and bottom face of lower
disc.

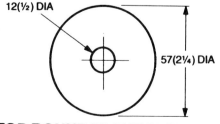

12(½) DIA

57(2¼) DIA

TOP ROUNDABOUT SPINDLE DISC
6(¼) PLYWOOD

21 Now cut top spindle disc. This keeps roundabout
in place on centre spindle.

42

22 From grid given mark on paper or card shape of horse. Cut out and transfer shape on to plywood. 3 horses are required.

32 Use coping saw to cut out horses. You will need to turn saw handle and blade several times to get round all curves.

24 After cutting out horses smooth all rough edges with glass paper and drill small holes for suspension cords.

25 Before mounting horses on roundabout paint as required.

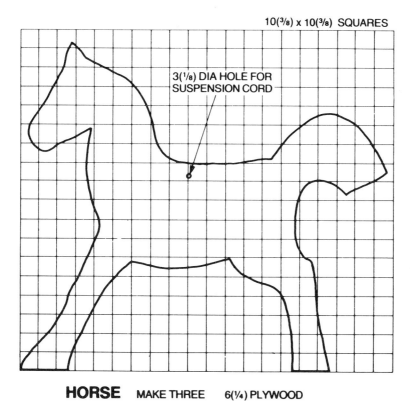

10(³/₈) x 10(³/₈) SQUARES

3(¹/₈) DIA HOLE FOR SUSPENSION CORD

HORSE MAKE THREE 6(¼) PLYWOOD

26 **Final Assembly:**
Check each piece for sharp edges and glass paper all over. Painting or varnishing should be done before the wheels or roundabout are attached to chassis. Insert axle and fix main wheels. Fit central roundabout spindle into place and glue into chassis mounting block hole. Fit roundabout on to spindle and glue spindle disc on to top of central spindle. Make sure that roundabout can turn freely. Candle wax on spindle will help smooth movement. Bottom disc should now touch only one wheel. Tie horses on to roundabout using nylon cord.

The roundabout is now ready for action.

12(½) DIA

238(9³/₈)

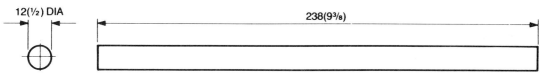

CENTRAL ROUNDABOUT SPINDLE
NOTE: GLUE ENDS TO TOP ROUNDABOUT SPINDLE DISC
AND MAIN CHASSIS ONLY

43

Rocking Horse

Of all Victorian toys the rocking horse must surely be the most treasured possession. Victorian rocking horses with their carved bodies and beautifully carved rockers are a thing of beauty, displaying the skill and artistry of the craftsman.

This little rocking horse, or perhaps Shetland pony, comes from a much humbler stable. However, its simplicity and strength will, I hope, endear it to many children who have a great love for their four-footed friends.

Cutting List

BODY SIDE MEMBERS*	2 off	515 mm (20$\frac{3}{8}$ in.) ×200 mm (7$\frac{7}{8}$ in.) ×9 mm ($\frac{3}{8}$ in.)
BODY FORMERS*	2 off	181 mm (7$\frac{1}{8}$ in.) ×165 mm (6$\frac{1}{2}$ in.) ×9 mm ($\frac{3}{8}$ in.)
	2 off	172 mm (6$\frac{3}{4}$ in.) ×165 mm (6$\frac{1}{2}$ in.) ×9 mm ($\frac{3}{8}$ in.)
HEAD*	1 off	350 mm (14 in.) ×350 mm (14 in.) ×12 mm ($\frac{1}{2}$ in.)
TAIL*	1 off	275 mm (11 in.) ×250 mm (10 in.) ×9 mm ($\frac{3}{8}$ in.)
LEGS	4 off	310 mm (12$\frac{1}{2}$ in.) ×115 mm (4$\frac{1}{2}$ in.) ×22 mm ($\frac{7}{8}$ in.)
BACK*	1 off	455 mm (17$\frac{7}{8}$ in.) ×108 mm (4$\frac{1}{4}$ in.) ×9 mm ($\frac{3}{8}$ in.)
ROCKERS	2 off	1120 mm (44 in.) ×165 mm (6$\frac{1}{2}$ in.) ×22 mm ($\frac{7}{8}$ in.)
STRETCHERS	2 off	270 mm (10$\frac{5}{8}$ in.) ×50 mm (2 in.) ×22 mm ($\frac{7}{8}$ in.)
FOOT RESTS	2 off	130 mm (5$\frac{1}{8}$ in.) ×65 mm (2$\frac{1}{2}$ in.) ×22 mm ($\frac{7}{8}$ in.)
SEAT (chipboard)	1 off	190 mm (7$\frac{1}{2}$ in.) ×140 mm (5$\frac{1}{2}$ in.) ×19 mm ($\frac{3}{4}$ in.)

*=plywood

Other materials

Black plastic or leather strip for harness, fur fabric, screws, panel pins, upholstery nails, wood glue, varnish.

Rocking Horse
construction details

1 The two sides are held together with 4 formers. 2 formers fit inside the body to give rigidity. 2 make up the back and front.

2 All formers are the same shape but dimensions vary so careful attention should be paid to dimension chart.

FORMER	DIM 'A'	DIM 'B'	DIM 'C'	DIM 'D'
FRONT	12(½)	40(1⅝)	99(3⅞)	181(7⅛)
SECOND	12(½)	20(¾)	90(3½)	172(6¾)
THIRD	9(⅜)	30(1¼)	90(3½)	172(6¾)
REAR	9(⅜)	75(3)	99(3⅞)	181(7⅛)

3 Cut out formers.

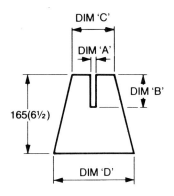

BODY FORMERS
9mm(⅜) THICK

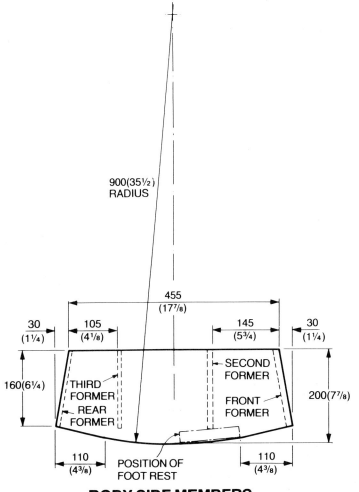

BODY SIDE MEMBERS
(showing position of formers and foot rest)
MAKE TWO, 9(⅜) PLYWOOD

4 Cut out and shape the 2 body side members. Place both in vice, plane edges to remove all saw marks. Make sure both side members are identical.

5 Clamp both side members to table or work bench. Grooves ('cut outs') at front and back must be made to take front and rear formers. Cut along groove lines with a tenon saw then carefully chisel off waste. If this is too difficult fit 90° plastic corner blocks instead, adjusting front and rear former sizes accordingly.

6 Assemble body 'dry' to check all pieces fit well.

7 An extra pair of hands is most welcome when holding the various pieces for gluing.

8 Glue sides to formers and panel pin them to give extra strength.

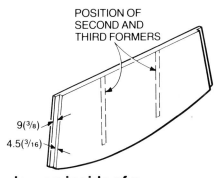

view on inside of a body side member showing cut outs for first and rear formers

9 From the grid given draw on to card the shapes of back and front legs. Cut out card and transfer shapes on to wood (pine).

10 Now cut legs to shape with coping saw and smooth all edges. The joint ('cut out') at top of outside of each leg (see diagram) is cut with tenon saw and allows legs to fit neatly and firmly on to horse's sides.

11 The legs are now glued and screwed on to body sides. The screws should be countersunk.

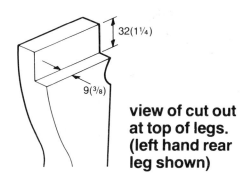

view of cut out at top of legs. (left hand rear leg shown)

32(1¼)

9(³⁄₈)

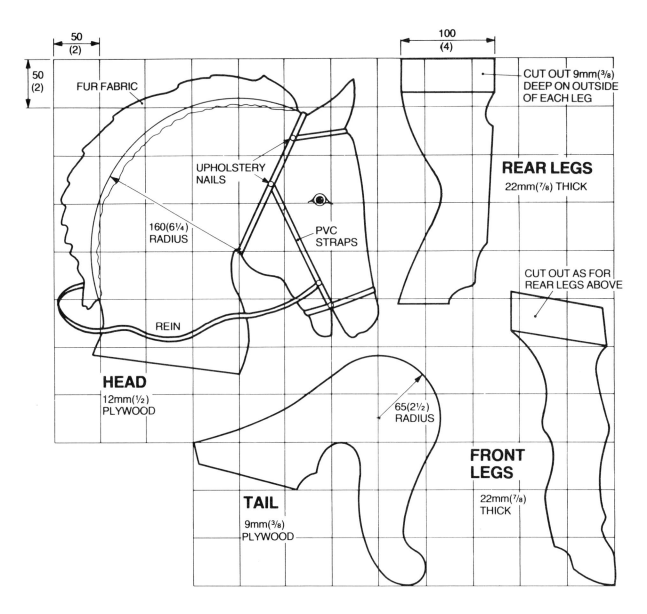

50 (2)

50 (2)

FUR FABRIC

UPHOLSTERY NAILS

160(6¼) RADIUS

PVC STRAPS

REIN

HEAD

12mm(½) PLYWOOD

65(2½) RADIUS

TAIL

9mm(³⁄₈) PLYWOOD

100 (4)

CUT OUT 9mm(³⁄₈) DEEP ON OUTSIDE OF EACH LEG

REAR LEGS

22mm(⁷⁄₈) THICK

CUT OUT AS FOR REAR LEGS ABOVE

FRONT LEGS

22mm(⁷⁄₈) THICK

12 The rider's foot-rests are made from pine and secured to body by screwing (2 screws to each rest) from inside. Use fairly long screws (e.g. 45 mm (1¾ in.)). Drill small 'pilot' screw holes into foot-rests before inserting main screws to screw into position.

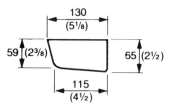

130 (5¹⁄₈)

59 (2³⁄₈)

65 (2½)

115 (4½)

FOOT RESTS

MAKE 2, 22mm(⁷⁄₈) THICK

13 Prepare horse's back cutting out slot for neck.

14 Glue and screw horse's back into place.

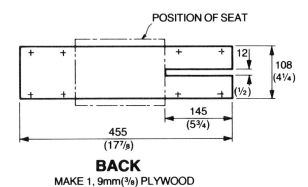

BACK
MAKE 1, 9mm(⅜) PLYWOOD

15 Following shapes on grid prepare card templates for head and tail. Transfer shapes on to plywood and cut out.

16 Smooth all edges of head and tail using glass paper.

17 Glue horse's tail into position in the rear and third former slots.

18 The reins are made from leather or black plastic strip as used for edging work tops, etc. available from Do-It-Yourself shops. Cut reins and fix with upholstery nails.

19 Make mane from fur fabric and glue to wood with contact adhesive.

20 Now glue horse's head into place. (Check fit before gluing.)

21 The seat is made from chipboard. Cut a piece of foam rubber to fit chipboard. Over this stretch a piece of chair covering material and secure to underside of seat with upholstery nails.

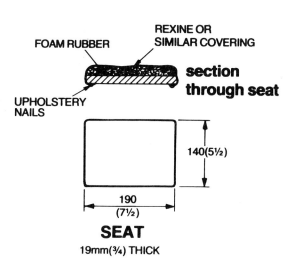

SEAT
19mm(¾) THICK

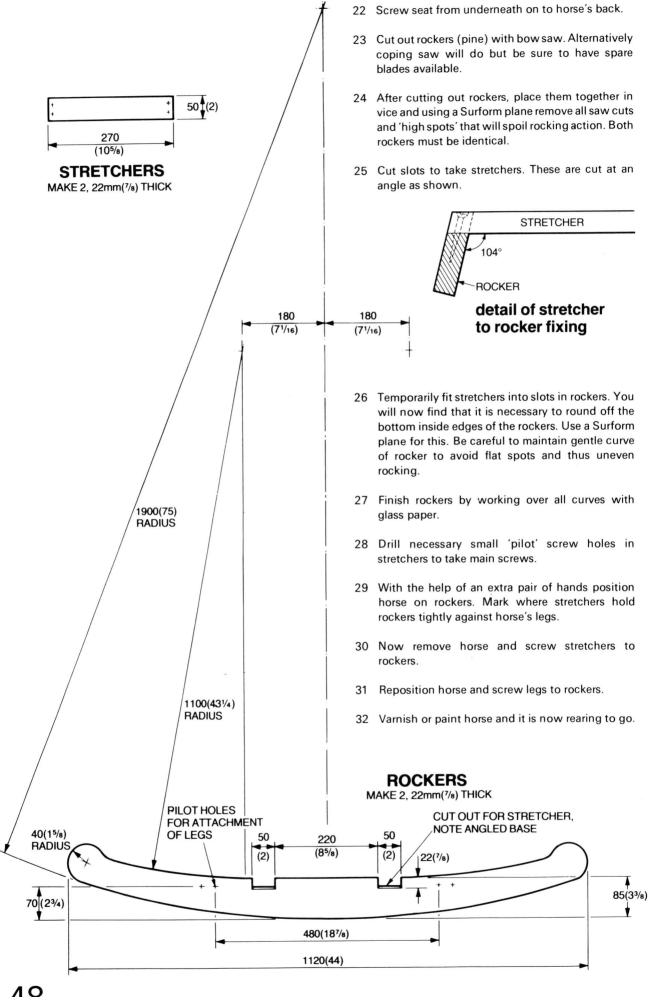

STRETCHERS
MAKE 2, 22mm(⁷⁄₈) THICK

50(2)

270
(10⁵⁄₈)

22 Screw seat from underneath on to horse's back.

23 Cut out rockers (pine) with bow saw. Alternatively coping saw will do but be sure to have spare blades available.

24 After cutting out rockers, place them together in vice and using a Surform plane remove all saw cuts and 'high spots' that will spoil rocking action. Both rockers must be identical.

25 Cut slots to take stretchers. These are cut at an angle as shown.

STRETCHER

104°

ROCKER

detail of stretcher to rocker fixing

180
(7¹⁄₁₆)

180
(7¹⁄₁₆)

26 Temporarily fit stretchers into slots in rockers. You will now find that it is necessary to round off the bottom inside edges of the rockers. Use a Surform plane for this. Be careful to maintain gentle curve of rocker to avoid flat spots and thus uneven rocking.

27 Finish rockers by working over all curves with glass paper.

28 Drill necessary small 'pilot' screw holes in stretchers to take main screws.

29 With the help of an extra pair of hands position horse on rockers. Mark where stretchers hold rockers tightly against horse's legs.

30 Now remove horse and screw stretchers to rockers.

31 Reposition horse and screw legs to rockers.

32 Varnish or paint horse and it is now rearing to go.

1900(75)
RADIUS

1100(43¼)
RADIUS

ROCKERS
MAKE 2, 22mm(⁷⁄₈) THICK

40(1⁵⁄₈)
RADIUS

PILOT HOLES
FOR ATTACHMENT
OF LEGS

CUT OUT FOR STRETCHER,
NOTE ANGLED BASE

50
(2)

220
(8⁵⁄₈)

50
(2)

22(⁷⁄₈)

70(2¾)

85(3⅜)

480(18⁷⁄₈)

1120(44)

48

Windmill

The working parts of this toy in no way resemble the mechanism of a real mill but perhaps its cams and cranks will inspire some young inventive minds to develop other ideas for machines.

This toy is quite difficult to construct.

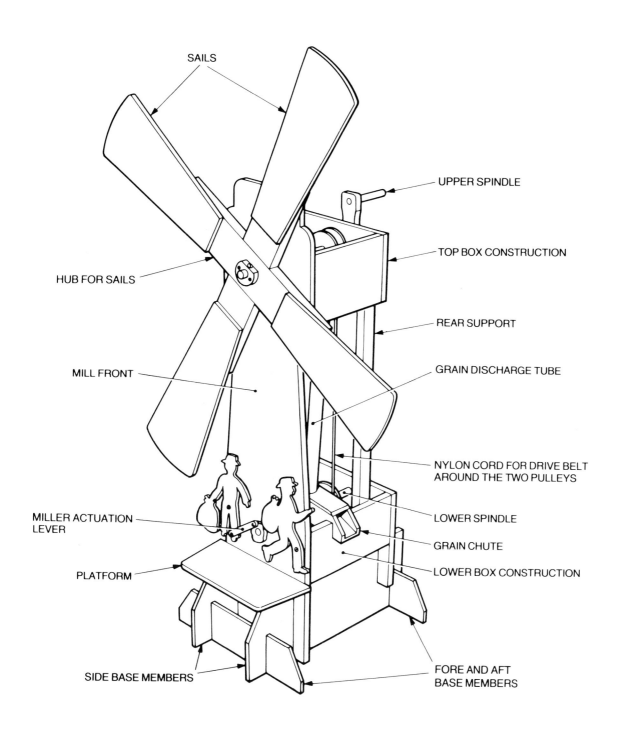

SAILS

UPPER SPINDLE

TOP BOX CONSTRUCTION

HUB FOR SAILS

REAR SUPPORT

GRAIN DISCHARGE TUBE

MILL FRONT

NYLON CORD FOR DRIVE BELT AROUND THE TWO PULLEYS

MILLER ACTUATION LEVER

LOWER SPINDLE

GRAIN CHUTE

PLATFORM

LOWER BOX CONSTRUCTION

SIDE BASE MEMBERS

FORE AND AFT BASE MEMBERS

Cutting List

MILL FRONT★	1 off	832 mm (32¾ in.) × 203 mm (8 in.) × 12 mm (½ in.)
SIDE BASE MEMBERS★	2 off	394 mm (15½ in.) × 152 mm (6 in.) × 12 mm (½ in.)
FORE AND AFT BASE MEMBERS★	2 off	318 mm (12½ in.) × 76 mm (3 in.) × 12 mm (½ in.)
PLATFORM★	1 off	235 mm (9¼ in.) × 114 mm (4½ in.) × 12 mm (½ in.)
LOWER BOX: back★	1 off	203 mm (8 in.) × 197 mm (7¾ in.) × 12 mm (½ in.)
sides★	2 off	203 mm (8 in.) × 95 mm (3¾ in.) × 12 mm (½ in.)
TOP BOX: back★	1 off	203 mm (8 in.) × 121 mm (4¾ in.) × 12 mm (½ in.)
sides★	2 off	152 mm (6 in.) × 121 mm (4¾ in.) × 12 mm (½ in.)
GRAIN TANK SUPPORT★	1 off	114 mm (4½ in.) × 57 mm (2¼ in.) × 12 mm (½ in.)
REAR SUPPORT COLUMNS	2 off	578 mm (22¾ in.) × 25 mm (1 in.) × 20 mm (¾ in.)
HUB FOR SAILS	2 off	381 mm (15 in.) × 70 mm (2¾ in.) × 20 mm (¾ in.)
SAILS★	4 off	495 mm (19½ in.) × 152 mm (6 in.) × 12 mm (½ in.)
MILL WORKERS★	1 off	300 mm (12 in.) × 180 mm (7 in.) × 9 mm (⅜ in.)
RETAINING RING★	1 off	54 mm (2⅛ in.) × 54 mm (2⅛ in.) × 12 mm (½ in.)
CRANKS, ROCKERS, ETC.★	1 off	300 mm (12 in.) × 100 mm (4 in.) × 12 mm (½ in.)
GRAIN CHUTE★: sides	2 off	121 mm (4¾ in.) × 50 mm (2 in.) × 9 mm (⅜ in.)
end	1 off	50 mm (2 in.) × 50 mm (2 in.) × 9 mm (⅜ in.)
top and bottom	2 off	121 mm (4¾ in.) × 50 mm (2 in.) × 9 mm (⅜ in.)
UPPER SPINDLE	1 off	330 mm (13 in.) × 12 mm (½ in.) diameter dowel
LOWER SPINDLE	1 off	254 mm (10 in.) × 12 mm (½ in.) diameter dowel
DRIVE PULLEYS	1 off	128 mm (5 in.) × 128 mm (5 in.) × 9 mm (⅜ in.)
	1 off	128 mm (5 in.) × 115 mm (4½ in.) × 6 mm (¼ in.)

★ = plywood

Other materials

Plastic tube (grain discharge tube), nylon cord, washers, elastic band, plastic container (grain bin) and wood glue.

Windmill
construction details

1 Before starting to make this toy, study carefully the diagrams of all the different parts and identify them on the main drawing.

2 Shape the mill front. Cut slots and drill holes as shown.

3 The slots at the base take the side base members. Slots should always be cut to allow a tight fit.

4 Cut out 2 side base members.

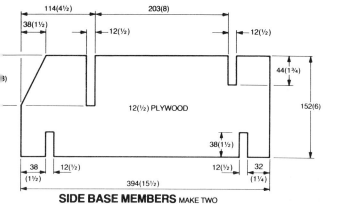

SIDE BASE MEMBERS MAKE TWO

5 Cut out fore and aft members.

6 Now slot these pieces together to get an overall impression of the windmill.

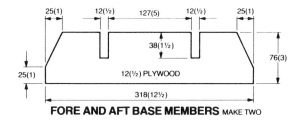

FORE AND AFT BASE MEMBERS MAKE TWO

7 Cut and shape platform. This fits at front on top of side members.

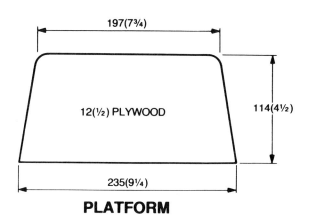

PLATFORM

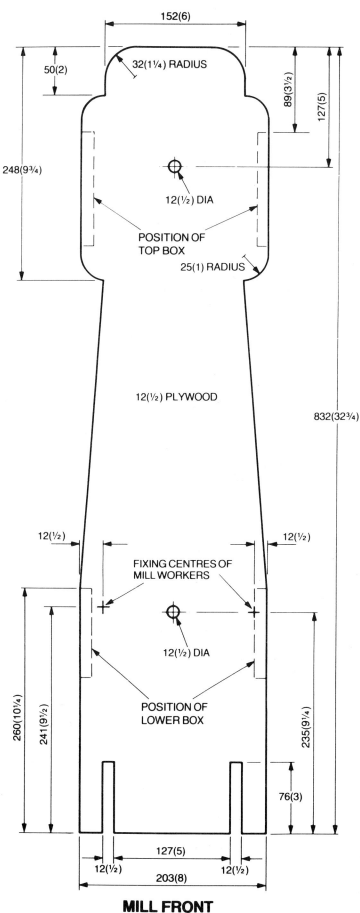

MILL FRONT

51

8   The lower box holds the grain chute and also the spindle which moves mill workers. Its other function is to hold rear support columns. Make up box screwing support columns into place. Then glue and screw box to mill front as shown.

9   The top box is also glued and screwed to mill front and screwed to rear support columns in the same way. This box holds windmill sail spindle on which is mounted 2 rockers which shake grain bin. Grain bin is held in place by a small piece of plywood with a hole in it for the funnel of the grain bin.

LOWER BOX CONSTRUCTION
12(½) PLYWOOD

TOP BOX CONSTRUCTION
12(½) PLYWOOD

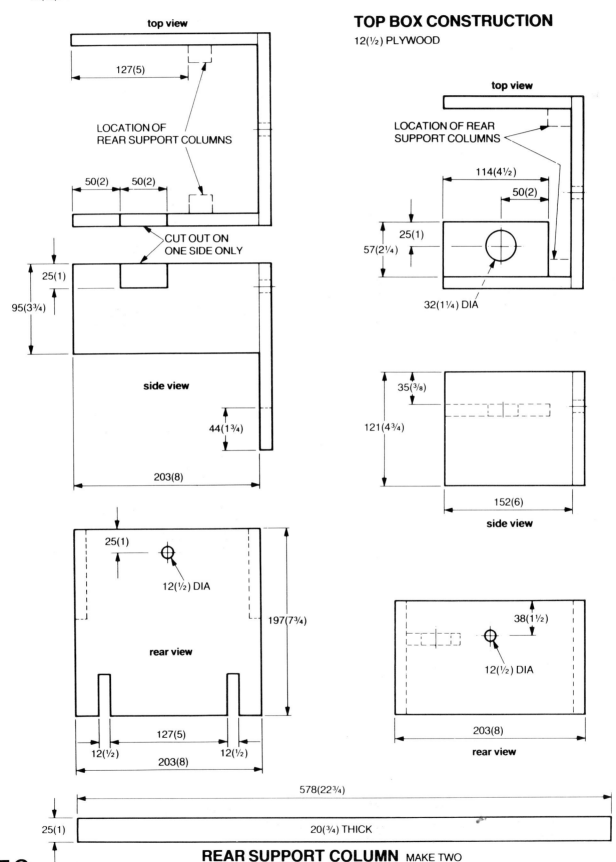

REAR SUPPORT COLUMN MAKE TWO

10 The grain bin is a plastic luncheon box with a hole cut in the bottom and a plastic funnel glued in place. The grain discharge tube which takes grain to the grain chute is made of plastic tube. The tube used by electricians for running cables in is suitable and available in most electrical shops.

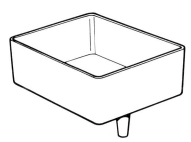

102(4) x 102(4) x 50(2) DEEP PLASTIC CONTAINER WITH THE END OF A PLASTIC FUNNEL BONDED THROUGH ITS BASE TO LINE UP WITH GRAIN DISCHARGE TUBE

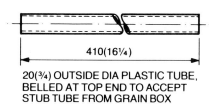

410(16¼)

20(¾) OUTSIDE DIA PLASTIC TUBE, BELLED AT TOP END TO ACCEPT STUB TUBE FROM GRAIN BOX

GRAIN DISCHARGE TUBE

11 The lower and upper spindles are then made. The drive pulleys are made from plywood (3 pieces of ply to each pulley, the middle piece having the smaller diameter 6 mm ($\frac{1}{4}$ in.) to allow groove for drive belt). The least expensive tool for making the pulley discs is the tank cutter or hole saw which is sold in sets. To prevent the nylon drive belt from slipping on drive pulleys cut and glue a piece of wide elastic band in pulley grooves.

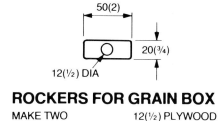

50(2)

20(¾)

12(½) DIA

ROCKERS FOR GRAIN BOX
MAKE TWO   12(½) PLYWOOD

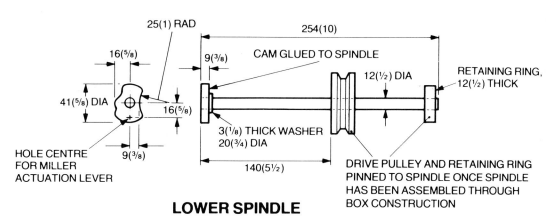

25(1) RAD

254(10)

16(⅝)

9(⅜)   CAM GLUED TO SPINDLE

12(½) DIA

RETAINING RING, 12(½) THICK

41(⅝) DIA

16(⅝)

3(⅛) THICK WASHER 20(¾) DIA

HOLE CENTRE FOR MILLER ACTUATION LEVER

9(⅜)

140(5½)

DRIVE PULLEY AND RETAINING RING PINNED TO SPINDLE ONCE SPINDLE HAS BEEN ASSEMBLED THROUGH BOX CONSTRUCTION

LOWER SPINDLE

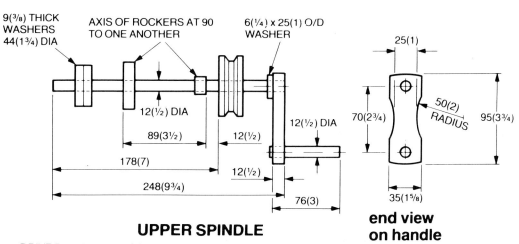

9(⅜) THICK WASHERS 44(1¾) DIA

AXIS OF ROCKERS AT 90 TO ONE ANOTHER

6(¼) x 25(1) O/D WASHER

25(1)

12(½) DIA

89(3½)

12(½)

12(½) DIA

70(2¾)

50(2) RADIUS

95(3¾)

178(7)

248(9¾)

12(½)

76(3)

35(1⅝)

end view on handle

UPPER SPINDLE
DRIVE PULLEY AND ROCKERS PINNED TO SPINDLE ONCE SPINDLE HAS BEEN ASSEMBLED THROUGH BOX CONSTRUCTION

53

12 Push the spindles through the spindle holes in their respective boxes and check spindle turns freely before attaching and gluing the drive pulleys, rockers, cranks, etc. A little candle wax provides a good lubricant.

13 Glue and screw handle to upper spindle.

14 Tie nylon cord as drive belt between upper and lower pulleys and check that mechanism works smoothly.

15 Now using coping saw cut out mill workers. Drill holes as shown and screw workers to mill front. Use washers or plastic tube spacers so men are clear of mill front.

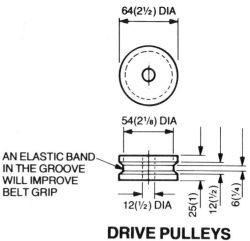

64(2½) DIA

54(2⅛) DIA

AN ELASTIC BAND IN THE GROOVE WILL IMPROVE BELT GRIP

12(½) DIA

25(1) 12(½) 6(¼)

DRIVE PULLEYS
MAKE TWO

10(³⁄₈) x 10(³⁄₈) SQUARES   **MILL WORKERS** 9(³⁄₈) PLYWOOD

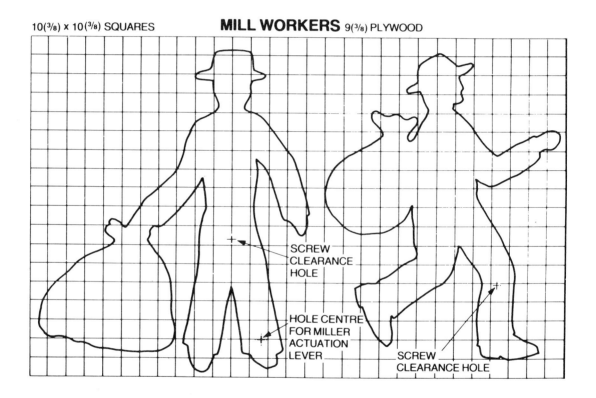

SCREW CLEARANCE HOLE

HOLE CENTRE FOR MILLER ACTUATION LEVER

SCREW CLEARANCE HOLE

16 Fix actuation lever on to leg of miller's boy and spindle cam, turn spindle and check all moves freely. Now attach miller. He moves up and down as his sack is pushed by rotating cam.

76(3)

12(½)

SCREW CLEARANCE HOLES

MILLER ACTUATION LEVER
9(³⁄₈) PLYWOOD

54

17 Now make grain chute. The grain discharge tube fits firmly into hole in top of chute. Fit chute on to side of lower box and glue.

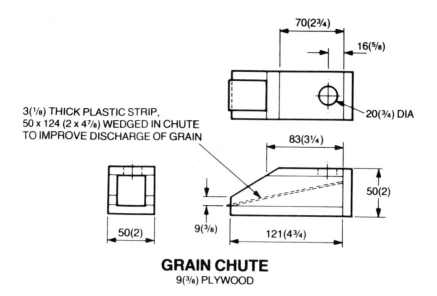

3(⅛) THICK PLASTIC STRIP,
50 x 124 (2 x 4⅞) WEDGED IN CHUTE
TO IMPROVE DISCHARGE OF GRAIN

70(2¾)
16(⅝)
20(¾) DIA
83(3¼)
50(2)
50(2)
9(⅜)
121(4¾)

GRAIN CHUTE
9(⅜) PLYWOOD

18 The windmill sails are held to the upper spindle by a hub. The crosses of the hub fit together with a halving joint. The hub is held in place on upper spindle by a screw as shown.

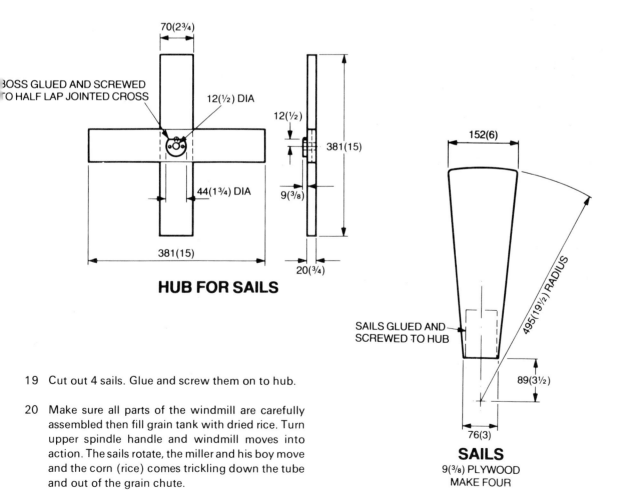

70(2¾)

BOSS GLUED AND SCREWED
TO HALF LAP JOINTED CROSS

12(½) DIA
44(1¾) DIA
381(15)

12(½)
381(15)
9(⅜)
20(¾)

HUB FOR SAILS

152(6)

495(19½) RADIUS

SAILS GLUED AND
SCREWED TO HUB

89(3½)

76(3)

SAILS
9(⅜) PLYWOOD
MAKE FOUR

19 Cut out 4 sails. Glue and screw them on to hub.

20 Make sure all parts of the windmill are carefully assembled then fill grain tank with dried rice. Turn upper spindle handle and windmill moves into action. The sails rotate, the miller and his boy move and the corn (rice) comes trickling down the tube and out of the grain chute.

6-Wheel Lorry (Truck)

This sturdy little lorry is ideal for carrying heavy loads and will take a child sitting or riding on it.

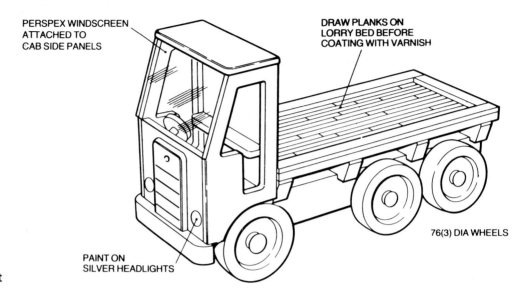

PERSPEX WINDSCREEN ATTACHED TO CAB SIDE PANELS

DRAW PLANKS ON LORRY BED BEFORE COATING WITH VARNISH

76(3) DIA WHEELS

PAINT ON SILVER HEADLIGHTS

Cutting List

CHASSIS SIDES	2 off	333 mm (13$\frac{1}{8}$ in.) × 47 mm (1$\frac{7}{8}$ in.) × 22 mm ($\frac{7}{8}$ in.)
CHASSIS CROSS PIECES	4 off	133 mm (5$\frac{1}{4}$ in.) × 25 mm (1 in.) × 16 mm ($\frac{5}{8}$ in.)
LORRY BED★	1 off	280 mm (11 in.) × 133 mm (5$\frac{1}{4}$ in.) × 9 mm ($\frac{3}{8}$ in.)
LORRY BED STRIPS	1 off	690 mm (28 in.) × 16 mm ($\frac{5}{8}$ in.) × 6 mm ($\frac{1}{4}$ in.)
BUMPER	1 off	137 mm (5$\frac{3}{8}$ in.) × 41 mm (1$\frac{5}{8}$ in.) × 22 mm ($\frac{7}{8}$ in.)
CAB PARTS:		
roof★	1 off	140 mm (5$\frac{1}{2}$ in.) × 60 mm (2$\frac{3}{8}$ in.) × 9 mm ($\frac{3}{8}$ in.)
rear★	1 off	111 mm (4$\frac{3}{8}$ in.) × 127 mm (5 in.) × 9 mm ($\frac{3}{8}$ in.)
floor★	1 off	111 mm (4$\frac{3}{8}$ in.) × 67 mm (2$\frac{5}{8}$ in.) × 9 mm ($\frac{3}{8}$ in.)
front bulkhead★	1 off	111 mm (4$\frac{3}{8}$ in.) × 86 mm (3$\frac{3}{8}$ in.) × 9 mm ($\frac{3}{8}$ in.)
seat★	1 off	111 mm (4$\frac{3}{8}$ in.) × 20 mm ($\frac{3}{4}$ in.) × 9 mm ($\frac{3}{8}$ in.)
radiator★	1 off	70 mm (2$\frac{3}{4}$ in.) × 64 mm (2$\frac{1}{2}$ in.) × 9 mm ($\frac{3}{8}$ in.)
side panels★	2 off	162 mm (6$\frac{3}{8}$ in.) × 76 mm (3 in.) × 9 mm ($\frac{3}{8}$ in.)
steering wheel shaft	1 off	38 mm (1$\frac{1}{2}$ in.) × 9 mm ($\frac{3}{8}$ in.) diameter dowel
steering wheel★	1 off	32 mm (1$\frac{1}{4}$ in.) × 32 mm (1$\frac{1}{4}$ in.) × 9 mm ($\frac{3}{8}$ in.)
windscreen (Perspex)	1 off	111 mm (4$\frac{3}{8}$ in.) × 85 mm (3$\frac{3}{8}$ in.) × 3 mm ($\frac{1}{8}$ in.)

★=plywood

Other materials

Six 76 mm (3 in.) diameter wheels, 3 axles, spring axle clips, wood glue, screws.

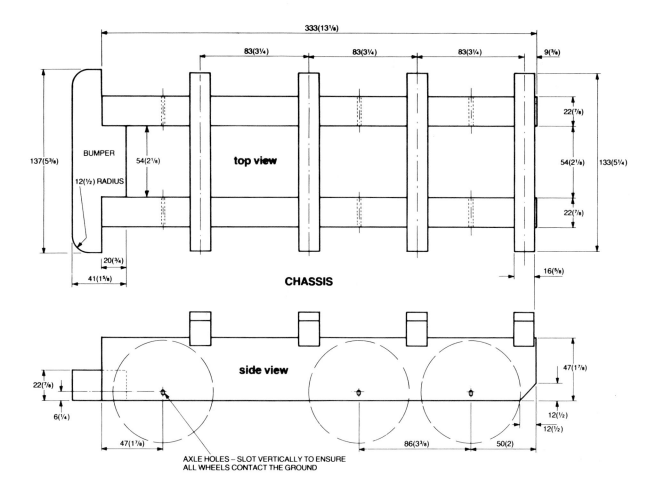

CHASSIS

top view

side view

AXLE HOLES – SLOT VERTICALLY TO ENSURE
ALL WHEELS CONTACT THE GROUND

Flat Bed 6-Wheel Lorry
construction detail

1 As with all vehicles first construct the chassis.

2 Take the 2 chassis sides and mark position of axle
   holes.

3 Hold both pieces together with a clamp or tape
   and drill axle holes. As with all axle holes the drill
   must be held at 90° to the chassis side. If possible
   use a vertical drill stand with electric (or hand)
   drill. If not find someone who can watch and
   check you do not drill out of vertical.

4 Enlarge the axle holes a little vertically as shown to
   ensure that all wheels touch the ground when lorry
   is assembled.

5 The 2 chassis sides are fixed together by 4 cross
   frames.

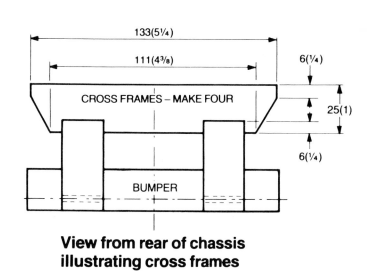

CROSS FRAMES – MAKE FOUR

BUMPER

View from rear of chassis
illustrating cross frames

6   Clamp the 4 cross frames together and mark angle cuts and slots. Place in vice and cut using tenon saw, removing waste pieces from slots with chisel.

7   Shape bumper.

8   Place all cross frames on to chassis sides in correct positions. Insert axles in axle holes. Check every piece fits correctly. Then glue together adding bumper. For increased strength screw cross frames and bumper to chassis sides.

9   Now construct cab. This is built from plywood with Perspex windscreen.

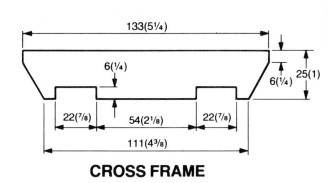

CROSS FRAME

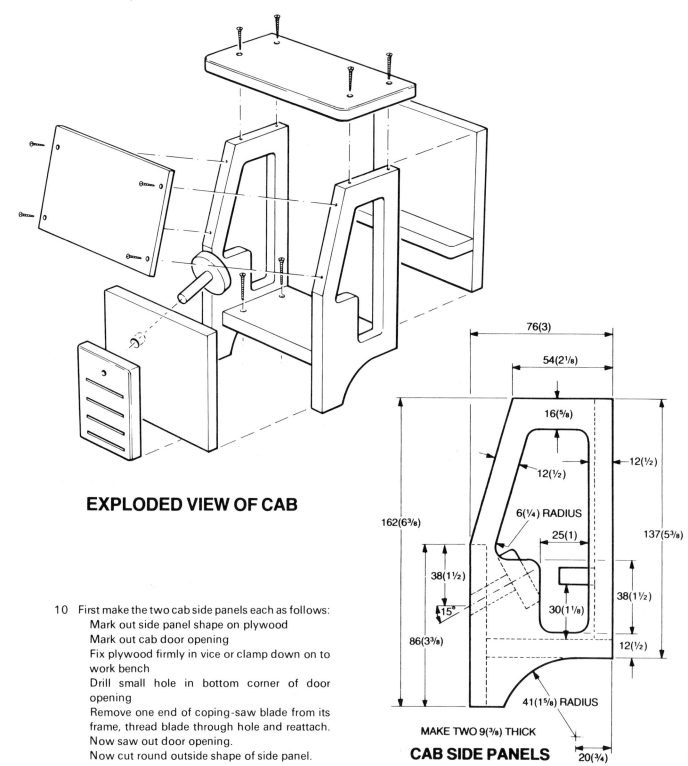

EXPLODED VIEW OF CAB

10 First make the two cab side panels each as follows:
    Mark out side panel shape on plywood
    Mark out cab door opening
    Fix plywood firmly in vice or clamp down on to work bench
    Drill small hole in bottom corner of door opening
    Remove one end of coping-saw blade from its frame, thread blade through hole and reattach. Now saw out door opening.
    Now cut round outside shape of side panel.

MAKE TWO 9(³⁄₈) THICK

CAB SIDE PANELS

58

11 Cut steering wheel from 9 mm ($\frac{3}{8}$ in.) plywood. The shaft from 9 mm ($\frac{3}{8}$ in.) dowel. Drill hole in centre of steering wheel for shaft as shown. Glue shaft into steering wheel.

12 Take front bulkhead and drill 9 mm ($\frac{3}{8}$ in.) hole at angle shown and glue in steering wheel.

13 Take cab parts (floor, rear wall, seat, side panels, front bulkhead with steering wheel) and glue and screw together. Do *not* attach roof yet.

14 Secure cab to lorry chassis by screwing cab floor to chassis sides.

15 Screw on cab roof.

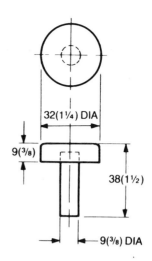

STEERING WHEEL

CAB PANELS – 1 off each – 9($\frac{3}{8}$) thick			
Panel	**Length**	**Width**	**Notes**
ROOF	60(2$\frac{3}{8}$)	140(5$\frac{1}{2}$)	6($\frac{1}{4}$) RADIUS ON FRONT CORNERS – ROUND OFF TOP EDGES
REAR	127(5)	111(4$\frac{3}{8}$)	
FLOOR	67(2$\frac{5}{8}$)	111(4$\frac{3}{8}$)	
FRONT BULKHEAD	86(3$\frac{3}{8}$)	111(4$\frac{3}{8}$)	
SEAT	20($\frac{3}{4}$)	111(4$\frac{3}{8}$)	
RADIATOR	70(2$\frac{3}{4}$)	64(2$\frac{1}{2}$)	9($\frac{3}{8}$) RADIUS ON TOP CORNERS – ROUND OFF TOP AND SIDE FRONT EDGES

16 Glue radiator on to front of bulkhead drawing lines as shown on main diagram for greater realism.

17 Cut Perspex windscreen to size with tenon saw taking care it does not crack. Drill a hole in each corner and screw into place.

18 The lorry bed is made from plywood and is screwed on to chassis sides. Black lead pencil is used to give imitation planking which is varnished.

19 Glue and screw small strips of wood round bed to prevent cargo slipping off.

20 For extra realism, number plates and fuel tank can be added.

21 Finish off by painting or varnishing model.

22 Fit axles and wheels. Model is now ready for action.

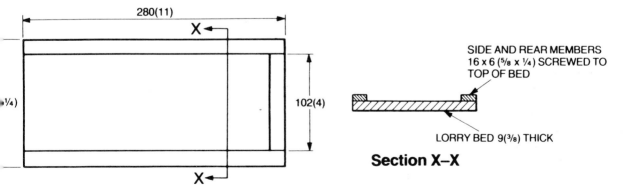

LORRY BED ASSEMBLY

Go-Cart and Trailer

This is a great favourite for outdoors and is constructed to give years of hard wear. Small pram or pushchair wheels can easily be fitted to this model.

Cutting List

GO-CART BASE★	1 off	960 mm (37¾ in.) × 380 mm (15 in.) × 9 mm (⅜ in.)
TRAILER BASE★	1 off	515 mm (20½ in.) × 285 mm (11¼ in.) × 9 mm (⅜ in.)
TRAILER SIDES★	2 off	280 mm (11 in.) × 152 mm (6 in.) × 9 mm (⅜ in.)
GO-CART SIDES★	2 off	355 mm (14 in.) × 152 mm (6 in.) × 9 mm (⅜ in.)
GO-CART CENTRE chassis member	1 off	1050 mm (41¼ in.) × 44 mm (1¾ in.) × 41 mm (1⅝ in.)
chassis side members	2 off	355 mm (14 in.) × 44 mm (1¾ in.) × 41 mm (1⅝ in.)
TRAILER CENTRE chassis member	1 off	730 mm (28¾ in.) × 44 mm (1¾ in.) × 44 mm (1¾ in.)
chassis side members	2 off	280 mm (11 in.) × 44 mm (1¾ in.) × 22 mm (⅞ in.)
STEERING FRAME cross members	2 off	510 mm (20 in.) × 70 mm (2¾ in.) × 25 mm (1 in.)
STEERING FRAME spacers	4 off	70 mm (2¾ in.) × 50 mm (2 in.) × 25 mm (1 in.)
MUDGUARDS★	2 off	160 mm (6¼ in.) × 152 mm (6 in.) × 6 mm (¼ in.)
BRAKE BATTEN	1 off	382 mm (15 in.) × 50 mm (2 in.) × 25 mm (1 in.)
DOWEL ROD (Go-Cart back support)	1 off	398 mm (15⅜ in.) × 20 mm (¾ in.) diameter dowel
DOWEL ROD (Trailer back support)	1 off	303 mm (12 in.) × 20 mm (¾ in.) diameter dowel
DOWEL ROD (to make towing pins)	1 off	152 mm (6 in.) × 20 mm (¾ in.) diameter dowel

★ = plywood

Other materials

Two 203 mm (8 in.) diameter wheels and axle rod, four
178 mm (7 in.) diameter wheels and axle rods, 115 mm
(4½ in.) × 9 mm (⅜ in.) diameter coach bolt, screws, glue,
rope.

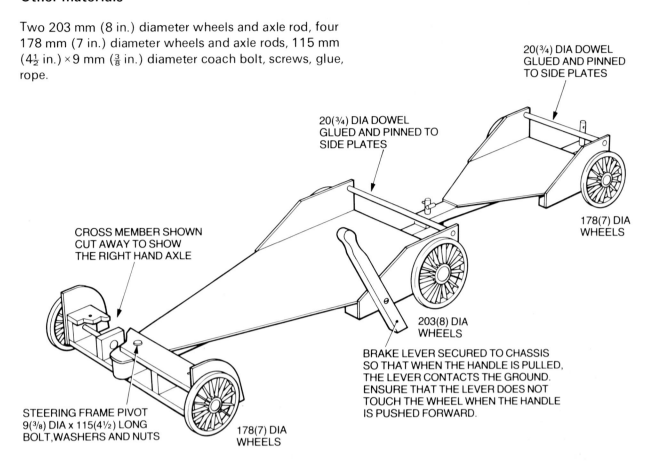

20(¾) DIA DOWEL
GLUED AND PINNED
TO SIDE PLATES

20(¾) DIA DOWEL
GLUED AND PINNED TO
SIDE PLATES

CROSS MEMBER SHOWN
CUT AWAY TO SHOW
THE RIGHT HAND AXLE

178(7) DIA
WHEELS

203(8) DIA
WHEELS

BRAKE LEVER SECURED TO CHASSIS
SO THAT WHEN THE HANDLE IS PULLED,
THE LEVER CONTACTS THE GROUND.
ENSURE THAT THE LEVER DOES NOT
TOUCH THE WHEEL WHEN THE HANDLE
IS PUSHED FORWARD.

STEERING FRAME PIVOT
9(⅜) DIA x 115(4½) LONG
BOLT, WASHERS AND NUTS

178(7) DIA
WHEELS

Go-Cart and Trailer
construction details

1   Cut out Go-Cart base. The crosses indicate where
    holes must be drilled for screwing on the 3 parallel
    chassis members. All holes must be countersunk
    to prevent screws protruding.

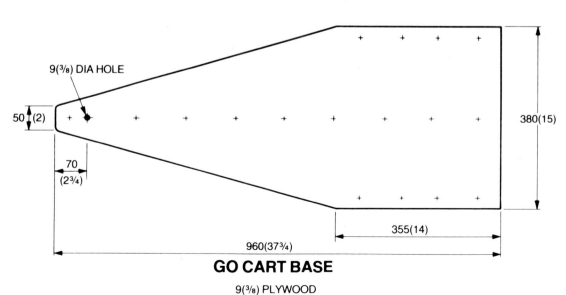

+ INDICATES FIXING POINTS

9(⅜) DIA HOLE

50 (2)

70
(2¾)

380(15)

355(14)

960(37¾)

GO CART BASE

9(⅜) PLYWOOD

61

2　Take central chassis member and round off front end. Drill hole and fit dowel pin at back end as shown.

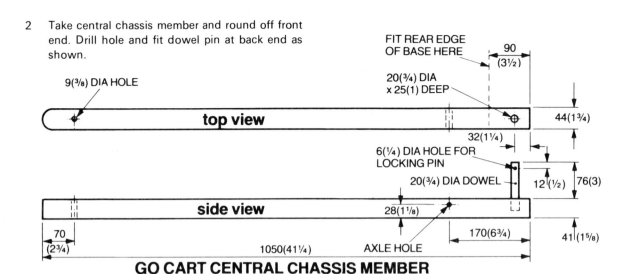

GO CART CENTRAL CHASSIS MEMBER

3　Clamp the 3 chassis members together and drill the back axle hole 9 mm (⅜ in.) diameter. Do not drill chassis members separately as the holes may not then align correctly.

4　Push axle through the 3 holes to align chassis members correctly. Position base board and screw chassis members in place.

5　Assemble Trailer base and chassis members in the same way. Drill Trailer hitch pin hole at front of central chassis member. Fit dowel pin at back to take a possible second trailer.

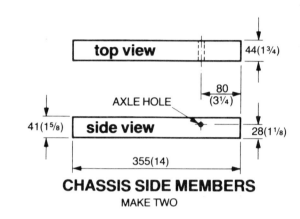

CHASSIS SIDE MEMBERS
MAKE TWO

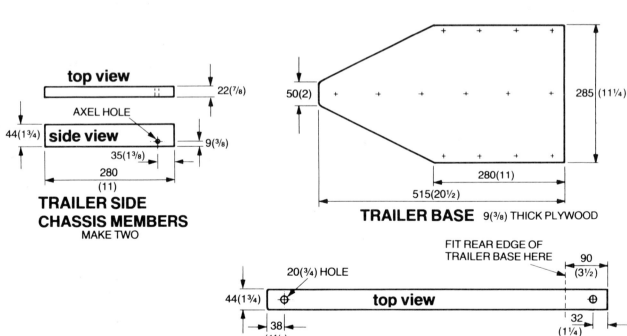

TRAILER SIDE CHASSIS MEMBERS
MAKE TWO

TRAILER BASE 9(⅜) THICK PLYWOOD

TRAILER CENTRAL CHASSIS MEMBER

6 Make a small locking pin as shown. This will prevent Trailer from accidentally separating from Go-Cart when moving. Drill hole 12 mm ($\frac{1}{2}$ in.) from top of Go-Cart chassis pin to take locking pin.

7 Shape Go-Cart and Trailer side plates, drill holes as shown and screw into position. The crosses show the position of screws which must be countersunk. Fit dowel rods at backs of Go-Cart and Trailer as shown, glue and pin. These act as back rests for driver and passenger.

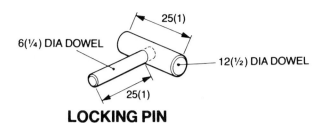

LOCKING PIN

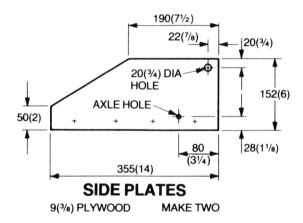

SIDE PLATES

9($\frac{3}{8}$) PLYWOOD   MAKE TWO

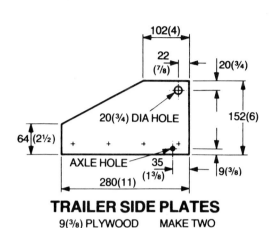

TRAILER SIDE PLATES

9($\frac{3}{8}$) PLYWOOD   MAKE TWO

8 Study main diagram carefully to understand how steering frame is constructed.

9 Take steering frame cross members and drill holes as shown.

10 Drill axle holes in the four steering frame spacers. A single axle does not run right through steering frame. Instead there is a half-axle on each side. These reach in as far as the second spacers as shown in cutaway on diagram.

11 Glue and screw spacers to cross frame members with axles in position. A spring cap is fitted on the inside of each half-axle.

12 Fit steering frame into position on front of Go-Cart. Now drill pivot hole through chassis.

13 Insert bolt and secure firmly. Make sure steering frame now pivots smoothly on chassis.

14 Cut out mudguards, glue and screw into place.

15 Attach towing rope to the 2 cord holes on steering frame.

16 Fit wheels and spring securing caps.

17 A brake should be added. This is a length of batten screwed on to the chassis side member as shown on opening diagram. A large diameter screw 64 mm (2$\frac{1}{2}$ in.) no. 10 should be used. The brake when pulled back will contact the ground and slow down the Go-Cart.

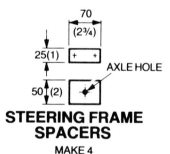

STEERING FRAME CROSS MEMBERS

20($\frac{3}{4}$) THICK   MAKE TWO

STEERING FRAME SPACERS

MAKE 4

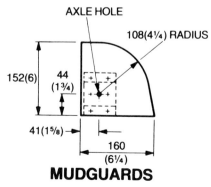

MUDGUARDS

6($\frac{1}{4}$) PLYWOOD   MAKE 2

63